A High
and
Holy Place

*A Mining Camp Church
at New Almaden*

A High
and
Holy Place

*A Mining Camp Church
at New Almaden*

by Gage McKinney

For thus says the high and lofty one who inhabits eternity,
whose name is holy: I dwell in the high and holy place,
and also with those who are contrite and humble in spirit,
to revive the spirit of the humble,
and to revive the heart of the contrite.
Isaiah 57:15

Cover illustration - "The Church on the Hill, New Almaden" by Milton
Lanyon, courtsey of Dr. John Faull

Published by The New Almaden County Quicksilver Park Association,
New Almaden Museum, P. O. Box 124, New Almaden, CA 95042

Printed by Pine Press, Sunnyvale, California
Second Printing, 1998

ISBN 0-9657994-0-9

The Cornish Emigrant's Song

Oh! the eastern winds are blowing;
The breezes seem to say,
'We are going, we are going,
To North Americay.

'There the merry bees are humming
Around the poor man's hive;
Parson Kingdom is not coming
To take away their tithe.

'There the yellow corn is growing
Free as the king's highway;
So, we're going, we are going
To North Americay.

'Uncle Rab shall be churchwarden,
And Dick shall be the squire,
And Jem, that lived at Norton,
Shall be leader of the quire;

'And I will be the preacher,
And preach three times a day
To every living creature
In North Americay.

R. S. Hawker
Cornish Ballads

Dedicated to

Dr. F. L. Harris,
Order of the British Empire

Foreword

Let me say at once that this is an impressive, important, and highly readable piece of research, and perhaps one of the first of its kind, by an author who is of Cornish descent himself, has visited Cornwall many times and even walked in the steps of the Wesleys. Out of his sensitive and sympathetic approach to the story of the Cornish contribution to quick-silver mining at New Almaden emerges an explanation of the nature of that "inner" strength which enabled the miners, their wives and families, to survive in a strange environment, not only of nature, but of people, Americans, Californios, Mexican, Chileans, Catholics and Protestants.

The narrative begins with an event, the attempt to hold a picnic in memory of a church that died, if only physically, but from it flows a new living history of a community which worshipped on the hill at New Almaden and from which it derived a spiritual discipline. The author deftly takes us back to the origins of Methodism in England, how John and Charles Wesley transformed the lives of ordinary people in a way that the Church of England did not, and how they built, especially in Cornwall, a new kind of church, both structurally and liturgically.

The chapters which follow are evocative of an age which has long disappeared, of circuit riders who ministered to the faithful at New Almaden, first in the open air, then in a chapel, the cost defrayed by personal subscription and grants from the mining company. The heart of the book is the author's graphic and colourful account of the organization of the Methodist community and its ministers, the pastors, the training of lay leaders and the weekly Bible classes for members of the congregation. In truth admission to these activities was not an easy option for members had to give proof of their sense of commitment. But the evidence is that lives were changed almost beyond belief when a mine captain would become the superintendent of the children's Sunday School, and ordinary miners could attend weekly classes in theology or the history of the Bible.

But inevitably, as the quicksilver mine at New Almaden began to run down, so the Cornish moved away to towns and cities like San Jose and worshipped there. By 1920 the chapel on the hill had become derelict. The intention of that gathering, the Church Day picnic, in May 1995, was to pay respect to the souls of the faithful departed of the Cornish who lived and worked there. Who they were, where they came from in Cornwall — are all in the book, enriched by personal accounts from descendants whom the author has known. Memories of that moving celebration two years ago may become blurred, but the author's book will revive them. For that is what history is about. Gage McKinney has made New Almaden's Methodist Church to live again in the present, even though its physical presence has disappeared. Such is the mystery of renewal and resurrection. No doubt the reader's heart will be "strangely warmed."

A. C. Todd
Warwickshire, England
1997

Preface

A history is an imaginative work, though it stands in a different relationship to facts than does a poem or a story. No history exists without a writer to set it down, to select the facts, and to take responsibility for interpreting them, as well as for any mistakes or errors in emphasis. While a writer spends countless hours alone, no one really writes alone. Written works are expressions of communities, of people of like minds or common experiences, and they resonate with the words of earlier writers. So as I release this brief account of the New Almaden church, I need to record the names of some who have helped, my partners in telling the story.

Many of the names, especially the names of those who participated in Methodist Church Day at New Almaden, are listed in the text. I would like to add that this story could not have been told without the commitment of the Methodists to their history and especially without the help of the Rev. Stephen Yale, Ph.D., director of archives for the California-Nevada Conference, the United Methodist Church. Steve was my friend and guide through much of the research. This story would not have been the same without the continuing support of the directors of the New Almaden County Quicksilver Park Association, who made Methodist Church Day possible and who have published this book. I especially thank Jo Young and Virginia Hammerness, who read the manuscript, and the association president, Kitty Monahan. Local pastors were an important support, including the Rev. M. David Wolf of Los Gatos United Methodist Church and the Rev. Glenda Thomas of Almaden Hills United Methodist Church. I had help, too, from the First United Methodist Church, San Jose. My thanks also to Janet Davis Engle, historian, Los Gatos United Methodist Church.

I am indebted to an army of family historians, especially the descendants of the Drew, Faull, James, Pearce, Tregoning and Wellington families, and to the descendants of William J. Trevorrow for loaning me his papers. I owe much to Russell Pearce, my friend and conduit to the collective memory of English Camp; and Clyde Arbucke, City Historian of San Jose. Thanks also to Leslie Masunaga, archivist of the History Museums of San Jose. I owe a debt to the California Room at the San Jose Public Library; to the Sourisseau Academy of San Jose State University; to the Green Library, Stanford University; and to the staff at the

Bancroft Library, University of California, Berkeley. Special thanks to the staff of the Flora Lamson Hewlett Library of the Graduate Theological Union, Berkeley. Finally, thanks to Linda Vaughn at the interlibrary loan desk and the staff of the Sunnyvale Public Library.

Much support has come from further afield. Thanks to Moira Tangye, director, The Cornish-American Connection, Murdoch House, Redruth, Cornwall; Dr. Kenneth E. Rowe, Drew University Library, Madison, New Jersey; and Dr. Marilyn Parr, research specialist, The Library of Congress, Washington, D. C. One of the pleasures of this work was studying in the Jefferson Reading Room. Thanks also to Maureen Williams of *Keltic Fringe* Magazine, my long-time publisher. I am especially grateful to the Rev. and Mrs. Thomas Shaw who gave my wife and me a tour of Gwennap Pit in Cornwall. The Rev. Shaw's books on Cornish Methodism were very valuable as well.

This brief work owes more than I can write to my wife, Ilka Weber, who read every draft, who stood beside me in the rain at Methodist Church Day, and who followed the trail of the Wesley's with me from London to the West Country and around Cornwall. It owes a great deal to Dr. A. C. Todd, a special friend to New Almaden, who inspired me with his books and who contributed the foreword to this one. It owes much, as do so many books about the Cornish, to Dr. Fred Harris, to whom it is dedicated. As founding president of the Cornwall Methodist History Society, and as scholar, teacher, dreamer and implementer, he has dedicated his life to Cornwall and the Cornish. During conversations in his home, Lambourne House at Mount Ambrose, and in letters and telephone conversations, he taught me the significance of the Methodist movement in the lives of working people. He taught me to admire the faithfulness, inner strength and courage of the Methodists — the qualities that Fred himself exemplifies.

Gage McKinney
Sunnyvale, California
1997

Table of Contents

NEW ALMADEN
QUICKSILVER COUNTY PARK
ASSOCIATION

The Methodist Church at New Almaden - *Those who climbed the hill to worship enjoyed a view to the east of the Santa Teresa Hills and the predominant Mount Hamilton Range (as pictured). To the north they saw the panorama of the Santa Clara Valley and San Francisco Bay. In the foreground are the cabins of the miners and their families. (L. Bulmore Collection, Sourisseau Academy, San Jose State University).*

1

Methodist Church Day, May 1995

When the Lord restored the fortunes of Zion
then were we like those who dream.
Psalm 126

It wasn't remarkable that on Saturday, May 13, 1995, volunteers hosted a church picnic at a county park in California, twelve miles south of San Jose. What was remarkable was that the particular church had not heard a sermon, sung a hymn or even opened its doors in more than eighty years. The picnic celebrated the life of the Methodist Episcopal Church that from about 1860 to 1914 served predominantly Cornish workers at North America's largest mercury mine at New Almaden, arguably the richest mine in California. About one hundred fifty attended, including people representing Methodist churches, the Methodist Historical Society, the California Cornish Cousins, and friends of the county park. Among them were about seventy-five descendants of families that attended the old church, people representing four generations, young and old, some who knew and some who were just learning about their Methodist heritage.

The picnic began as the dream of a museum docent who in an intuitive instant saw the history of the church not only in the images of its past, the church on the hill and the miners and families trooping up a trail as steep as a staircase, but also in images of the present, the descendants of the church gathered around the site where their forebears had worshipped. The New Almaden County Quicksilver Park Association, the volunteer group that helps to maintain trails in the 4,300 acre park and operates the museum, acknowledged the dream and organized a planning committee that included the association president, two Methodist ministers, a church historian and the docent. One of the committee's chief concerns was to provide shaded picnic tables because they imagined the event on a warm Spring day, dry brush, dusty trails. The planners imagined people gathered in the filtered sunlight beneath black oaks near the crown of the hill where the church once stood, and where they could enjoy a commanding view of the valley below, the great bay and the bridges. The organizers did not appreciate that the entire history of this church was against any plans that depended on the weather. The date of the picnic nearly coincided with the one hundred-twentieth anniversary of the dedication of a church building at the mining camp — a building that blew down its first winter. No one should have been surprised to wake on that May morning to the seamless black clouds and driving rain, one of the last storms of the wettest year in a generation.

Those who attended showed the tenacity of the Methodist pioneers and there were few cancellations. They drove to New Almaden along a partially washed-out road and passed by sandbags and other signs of recent flooding. They crowded in the New Almaden Community Club, where the moisture from their coats and umbrellas condensed on the windows. Talking excitedly, they passed along a make-shift serving line, collecting their Cornish pasties, apples, homemade cookies and sodas or beers. As more arrived and the rain continued steadily, the room filled beyond its capacity, every table crowded. People spilled out onto a deck where they sat at picnic tables and ate under umbrellas. Cora Trevorrow Bocks, a 98-year-old who had attended the church as a girl, sat under the eaves in her wheelchair and declined a seat inside — she wanted to sit with her family. Mary Trevorrow Frederick, 92, who also attended the church, huddled under an umbrella with her husband as she ate her pasty. No one complained, everyone made accommodations, everyone was companionable.

The descendants of the old church, from Mrs. Bocks down to a pair of toddlers named Faull, traced their lineage through the New Almaden settlement and back to Cornwall, the legendary land of Arthur, a Celtic land, a royal duchy and the southwest-most county of the United Kingdom. During the time of our history about 600 men, women and children were living in the English-speaking camp on Mine Hill at New Almaden and probably ninety per cent of them were Cornish. (Others were Irish, Scots, German and English.) A Cornish heritage is, at least in part, a mining heritage as suggested by an old expression, "A mine is a hole in the ground with a Cornishman at the bottom." The earliest workings in the old country date back a millennium before Christ and underground mining as we think of it began in Elizabethan times. For centuries Cornwall was Europe's largest supplier of tin. Copper mining began on a large scale in the eighteenth century.

The Cornish miner was once the foremost exponent of hardrock mining in the world and his specialized knowledge migrated across the oceans to the camps in the New World, Australia, Africa and Asia in the form of technology, especially Cornish steam engines and pumps, and in the form of skilled labor, miners themselves. As they emigrated the Cornish brought along their distinctive speech that bore remnants of an ancient Cornish language and that some Americans confused with Cockney. They brought their pasties and saffron buns, their love of singing and brass bands, and a sense of independence that well suited the American frontier. Their work at New Almaden was crucial to mining in the Far West because in their day mercury was the essential element in the refining of precious metals — there could be no gold rush or silver bonanza without it. This was all in the background, though, at Methodist Church Day, where everyone focused not on the mine but the community, not on the tribute miner but the preacher, not on the muckers but the choir.

The storm having put the plans in disarray, nothing came off as scheduled, yet the day unfolded according to its own mysterious sense of purpose. For the benefit of those sitting outside, a loudspeaker leaned in the doorway as Pastor David Wolf of the Los Gatos United Methodist Church said grace after almost everyone had eaten. Above the sound of dripping water the assembled were welcomed and heard historical talks. The Rev. Stephen Yale gave an account of the circuit riders, the early Methodist preachers, and as we listened to the rush of Los Alamitos Creek he reminded us, "They often died young, pierced by an arrow or drowned in a river." Later everyone joined in singing hymns by Charles Wesley, hymns often sung in the old church —"A Charge to Keep I Have," "O For A Thousand Tongues to Sing," "Jesus, United by Thy Grace," and "Love Divine, All Loves Excelling" — and it did not take a visionary to see the singers and hear in their voices the choirs of past generations. After the event, and with a break in the storm, many trooped to the New Almaden museum where they continued talking and sharing stories. It was not the day that anyone had dreamed or planned, yet in many ways it was a better one.

One day tells its tale to another, as the psalmist said, but often the stories of those days need interpreting. To understand what drew so many people to New Almaden despite the storm, and why this long-closed church is remembered by descendants to the third and fourth generations, requires analysis, something like the Jungian interpretation of a dream. We must go back to the founding of the Methodist movement, beginning with John and Charles Wesley, who are among the primary symbols. We must begin with some understanding of the shifting dreamscape of Cornwall with its fishing, choirs, hard-rock mining, and saints, and we must eventually come to Mine Hill at New Almaden, a settlement dominated by a mine, a school and a white-washed church.

Through the portals of the mine shaft, and up the wooden steps of the church, the Cornish immigrant entered America. By their Methodist discipline they became people of determination, men and women who could speak up and assume leadership, parents who could stress the value of education to their children. As the fortunes of mining dwindled, as we shall see, they left the mining camp for the city and found new professions and trades, but they did not forsake their Methodist faith. Through the urban churches this immigrant population moved into the mainstream of American society. The story of the New Almaden church is the story of these immigrants, and though it is not precisely the same as the story of our modern immigrants, the newest Americans who have arrived in the latter twentieth century, especially from Asia, Mexico and Central America, there are similarities. For all the immigrants to California there is no separating the spirit of the believer from the spirit of the citizen to be, the life that is dreamed of from the one that is lived.

2

A Wesleyan Heritage

Here is my servant, whom I uphold,
my chosen in whom my soul delights;
I have put my spirit upon him;
he will bring forth justice to the nations.
Isaiah, Chapter 42

In an era when we think of gentlemen riding, there could have been few better acquainted with the saddle than John Wesley, an Anglican priest who took a kingdom for his parish and whose teaching became a subtext to the story of New Almaden. In his own day there were none better acquainted with the British people than this Oxford don who knew the educated and elite, but who turned his attention towards the yet inchoate working class, the largely illiterate, backward, toiling poor who were the brute strength of the Industrial Revolution. His friend, Dr. Samuel Johnson, thought that Wesley knew more people, of more varied estates, than anyone else in Britain.

John Wesley was born in 1703, and his brother Charles in 1707, in the reign of Queen Anne. At five John effected his own rescue from a fire that destroyed the vicarage where his family lived, and the event grew in significance as he did himself. John attended Christ Church, Oxford, was ordained and became a fellow of Lincoln College, and Charles closely followed him. In 1729 John Wesley became the leader of a small group that Charles had gathered at Oxford. The group resolved to live a disciplined life, read the Greek New Testament together and receive communion weekly (in a day when quarterly was accepted practice). For seeming to be more religious than others, their follow students ridiculed them, calling them "the Sacramentalists," "Bible moths" or "enthusiasts," and other names. Charles Wesley wrote in his journal:

> I went to the weekly sacrament and persuaded two or three young students
> to accompany me and to observe the method of study prescribed by the
> University. This gained me the harmless name of Methodist.

These Oxford experiences were merely a beginning for John and Charles in their quests to live lives of spiritual authenticity. Both of them sailed across the Atlantic to take assignments in Georgia, but returned to England with little to show for their time away. Yet it was in crossing to America and in the immediately succeeding years that John became influenced by the Church of the Brethren, in Wesley's time known as Moravians, a Central European movement that aimed to recover the spirit and practice of the primitive Christians. Under their influence Wesley experienced a re-dedication or conversion at a Moravian meeting in London on 24 May 1738:

> In the evening I went very unwillingly to a [Moravian] society in Aldergate Street, where one was reading Luther's preface to the Epistle to the Romans. About a quarter before nine, while he was describing the changes which God works in the heart through faith in Christ, I felt my heart strangely warmed. I felt I did trust in Christ, Christ alone, for salvation; and an assurance was given me that He had taken away my sins, even mine, and saved me from the law of sin and death.

About the same time his brother Charles had a similar experience of "saving faith." The experience liberated John Wesley from the intense introspection that had marked his young life. A while later, in cooperation with George Whitefield, a member of the Oxford group, Wesley began preaching in the open air near Bristol to hundreds and thousands of people, many of them colliers, men regarded as uneducable. Turning all his energies to bringing salvation to others, Wesley swiftly became the focal point of a great awakening.

An awakening was needed. Remembering the horrors of the English civil war, the established church placed conformity above conviction, and its emphasis on reason ("the candle of the Lord") served to exaggerate the distance between an educated clergy and the working poor. Still focused on a passing agrarian society that revolved around the farmer and squire, the church had neglected the increasing population of laborers who had quitted the land for the industrial centers. Preaching had grown sterile and pluralism (the practice of a clergyman having multiple livings and "subletting" them) too often put poorer worshippers in the care of less committed or less capable curates. There was little about the church, save the sacraments themselves, that addressed the needs of the surging population of laboring people.

Seeing the need, Wesley and others went into the open air (and into those few churches that would welcome their style of preaching) to address the people who the established church had slighted. In industrial towns and mining districts they found audiences eager for good news. Wesley's genius, though, was not for preaching (as was the Rev. George Whitefield's) but for organization. He grouped the converted into small bands with appointed leaders so that the strong could encourage the weak, a cellular structure that has been imitated by many since, including the Abolitionists and trade unions. The early societies developed the character that came to be regarded as Methodist. As societies became established Wesley and other leaders visited to support them, to expound the scriptures, to make the gospel message comprehensible. They emphasized the individual's acceptance of a personal religion and the experiences of forgiveness and of God's power and presence. Every week in this work Wesley traveled usually two or three hundred miles; preached twenty or more times in public; answered thirty or forty letters; met privately with individuals; and worked on manuscripts for publication. This was the consistent pattern of his life for more than fifty years, ceaseless prayer, traveling and preaching until he died at eighty-nine.

As Wesley concentrated much of his efforts in London, the Midlands and the West Country around Bristol, it was not long before the movement gained a footing in Cornwall, closely connected to Bristol by sea. First Charles Wesley and then John rode beyond the Tamar River to support the new societies, and over the years John made thirty-two visits to Cornwall. In the old Duchy (as in other places) the Wesleys restored a religion of the heart sometimes house by house, and people responded by turning their houses into preaching places and eventually by building chapels.

Though the Cornish Methodist may have been few compared to the number of Methodists in other regions (the Cornish never comprised more than a tenth of Wesley's followers in Britain), they grew to dominance in their own small and insular land. In west Cornwall at a place called Gwennap Pit, the ruins of mine workings that had formed an amphitheater, Wesley preached to his largest gathering and recorded his generous reckoning in his journal, September 1781:

> About five in the evening I preached at Gwennap, I believe to two or three and twenty thousand were present, and I believe God enabled me to speak that even those who stood farthest off could hear distinctly. I think this is my *ne plus ultra*. I shall scarce see a larger congregation till we meet in the air.

Modified since Wesley's time, Gwennap Pit is still used for outdoor services.

Wesley found no sound on earth comparable to Cornish voices and he admired the Celtic tenacity. Rain no more dispersed the Cornish, he said, than it would a column of soldiers. The Cornish revered him and called him "Mr. Westley" — inadvertently inserting a "t" into his name. People who had heard Wesley preach, and especially their descendants, carried the impressions with them to the corners of the English-speaking world. A Cornish woman in California's Gold Country, Harriet Trengrove Barron, wrote the following in her Bible:

> Gwennap Pit was an open mine where John Wesley began in 1783 preaching to and converting thousands of Cornish people in the open air. He preached in Cornwall for forty years. He brought rebirth of pride in their work to the Cornish people, dignity to their living, tranquillity and understanding to their homes.

The Cornish Methodists' religious experience was not essentially different from that of Methodists in other parts of the United Kingdom or North America, or even from other Christians, but their expression of it revealed something of their distinct Celtic heritage. The emotional appeal of early Methodism, with its call to conversion, hymn singing and extemporaneous prayer, provided an outlet for religious expression that the Cornish had lacked since the Reformation. In the chapel and class meeting, along the pathway, in the fishing boat and in the depth of the mine, the Cornish sang Charles Wesley's hymns, full of allusions to the Scriptures, the Nicene Creed, and the older Catholicism that had once made Cornwall a land of saints.

Mining in Cornwall, with its hazards and terrors, long hours and miserable conditions, was brutalizing. (The same can be said of another principle Cornish occupation, deep sea fishing.) The life expectancy of a miner was only forty years. Methodism's message of deliverance through faith gave thousands the hope of a better life in another world, if not in this one, as it restored them to a community of believers. Its reassertion of the doctrine of Justification by Faith supplied a fitting paradigm for a time and place where a man, through the difficult and hazardous work of mining, could wrest his blessing from the earth. Methodism was an active faith that called for a belief in possibilities, and as such it helped men and women gain self-assurance and qualities of character that could enable them to seize their limited opportunities and turn them to account.

By the nineteenth century, especially in the western mining districts, emigration dominated Cornish life, offering many their best opportunity. Wherever the Cornish established themselves in America, near iron mines in New Jersey, close by lead and zinc mines in Wisconsin, beside the copper mines of Michigan's Keeweenaw Peninsula, in the badlands of Nevada, the deserts of Arizona or the foothills of the Sierra — anywhere the Cornish went Methodist societies took root in their homes and flowered into churches and congregations. In a Methodist church in the mining districts of California one was never far from Cornwall. In Grass Valley, where they once comprised sixty per cent of the population, the Cornish swelled the numbers at the Methodist Episcopal Church and in brass and glass their names are preserved. In 1860 Cornish emigrants built The First Methodist Church at Soulsbyville, near Sonora, and their descendants worship there today. During the nineteenth and into the twentieth century Methodists in California came to recognize a distinctive Cornish element in their ranks, and nowhere was that element more evident than at New Almaden.

John Welsey preaching to the Cornish at Trewint - John and Charles Wesley made repeated visits to Cornwall. John wrote in his journal on 15 July 1745, "I never remember so great an awakening . . . from Trewint quite to the seaside." (From a watercolor by A. W. Gay).

3

The Santa Clara Circuit,
c. 1860 - 1871

My chains fell off, my heart was free,
I rose, went forth and followed Thee.
Charles Wesley, hymn

Probably Methodism came to Mine Hill at New Almaden as it came to innumerable frontier settlements, not as a result of planning, but the result of a purposefulness that only revealed itself over time. As it happened in other isolated places in the American West, it probably began on Mine Hill one Sunday when two or three families gathered in a single cabin for the reading of scripture and prayer. We cannot know in which house, but we can suppose that it was in the mid- to late-1850s when there were as many as twenty Cornish families settled at the mercury mine. In due time a minister came on horseback to support them, and since this is a California story, we can imagine him moving the preaching into the sunshine and open air, perhaps under one of those black oak trees, where some beyond the initial band could more easily hear the singing, remember the faith of their homeland and join in.

The organization that brought a circuit rider to Mine Hill was ideally suited for the American frontier because it developed out of a certain vagueness as does the crown of a tree. In America (as in England) the traveling preachers served "societies," small groups or congregations, along a "circuit," a prescribed route (vaguely circular) that might extend a few miles or hundreds of miles around. As the circuit riders pursued their strenuous ministry, many of the societies along the circuits grew strong enough to become "stations" with a preacher all their own. Thus, a circuit had elasticity, releasing congregations that grew into stations and extending to take up new ones as they emerged among the shifting populations of immigrants and pioneers. As Wesley devised the plan, and as it continued in America, a preacher usually continued on a circuit for a year or two and then moved to another.

Such admirable flexibility makes difficulties for anyone trying to trace the particular circuit that served New Almaden. This was the Santa Clara Circuit, established in 1854 as an extension of Methodist churches in Santa Clara and San Jose, but originally not including New Almaden. From some of the earliest records we know that the Rev. Isacc Owen, a venerated pioneer of Californian Methodism, took charge of the circuit in 1856 when it included Williams Chapel (four miles from Santa Clara), Saratoga, Eight Mile House on Monterey Road, Gilroy and Berryessa. The following year he took William Gafney (a recurring figure in our story) as an assistant, and between them they increased the membership on the circuit from just twenty-five to sixty-seven. Perhaps Owen's successors called at New Almaden, though litigation closed the mine in 1860, shrunk the population and probably discouraged initiative. As a result we cannot definitively locate a minister on Mine Hill before the Rev. R. R. Dunlap arrived to preach about 1861.

Most of our knowledge of the circuit comes from the ministers who built the primitive frontier churches. One minister stands out in relief because he built the first church at New Almaden, probably with his own hands, and because he left an account of his life and ministry. As shepherd to his flock the Rev. Edward Hazen employed the proven methods of revivals, soul-stirring prayer and public conversions. His life's work, as he put it, was to bring salvation to the uttermost, and he came as a missionary to California to do it. Hazen's personal story reveals a sympathetic individual with an introspective side that made him anxious for his own soul, and it offers glimpses of the immediate scene as well as a broader picture of the life of an American Methodist in the mid-nineteenth century.

Hazen was born in Cortland County, New York in 1824. Reared in a church-going family, he used to climb into his small chair as if it were a pulpit and "preach" to his mother and sisters. The family fell away from the church through a succession of moves that took them to Ohio and Indiana. After his mother died of yellow fever, Hazen became (at least in his own mind) a wicked boy, though the only vice he specified was cursing at plow horses. Not wanting to condone sin, he leaves us to imagine what other temptations might have bedeviled a frontier boy. About this time he was revolted that Louisa, the older sister whom he idolized, had been converted, falling into the clutches of those he called "howling Methodists!"

Some months after her conversion, Louisa persuaded young Hazen to drive her to a Camp Meeting, a combination camp out and revival. He only intended to rest the horses before returning to the farm, but after twice harnessing and unharnessing them, he stayed for the afternoon sermon. He listened from the rear of the crowd, standing under a maple tree. The preacher seemed to know him, he remembered, and every word struck to his heart. When the sermon ended the preacher called the unconverted forward, but Hazen didn't move. Then after a moment he saw Louisa coming towards him, holding out her hand, big tears on her face. She lead him forward to a bench set aside for those in the throes of conversion, and as Hazen prayed, others gathered around him. At last he heard himself cry out, "God be merciful to me, a sinner!" In the stylized manner of the day he had been converted, embracing what only a short time before he had abhorred.

From that point the course for Hazen's life became clear, or at least as clear as it can be when a young man surrenders his life to a purpose beyond his conscious will. At home he and Louisa took turns reading scripture and leading their father and younger sister in prayer. At the local church he led prayer meetings when the lay preacher was away. Foreseeing that the Methodists would need better educated ministers than the ones he had known as a boy in the backwoods, Hazen began studying and became a carpenter to support himself as he continued his studies at Asbury University (now DePauw) in Greencastle, Indiana. At twenty-four, and before he could finish his degree, he accepted the position as assistant minister on a circuit in northern Indiana. Hazen rode to a schedule opposite the senior minister, preaching at eighteen appointed places during the course of three weeks, and having five days off in the fourth week. The following year he had his own appointment. "I studied my sermons on horseback," he said, "and did my general reading and that recommended in connection with the theological course at my nightly homes on my circuit." A few years later he married and requested a missionary assignment in California.

After arriving in San Francisco by sea in December 1852, Hazen served several appointments before accepting, late in 1863, an appointment to the Santa Clara Circuit, then including Berryessa, Evergreen and New Almaden. He felt he could "do a good work in restoring that charge to a good condition." "During our pastorate on the Santa Clara Circuit, consisting of two years," he wrote, "a gracious revival occurred at Berryessa, greatly strengthening the society in numbers and spirituality, and some at New Almaden. We built a neat little church at the latter place." The San Jose *Mercury* reported in April 1864:

New Church at Almaden - A Methodist Church has been erected at the mining village of New Almaden on the hill. It is twenty-two by thirty-two feet in size, and the congregation there worshipping will be under the pastoral charge of the Rev. E. A. Hazen.

(The little church that Hazen built does not seem to figure significantly in the story, as it doesn't appear again in the records and perhaps was soon out-grown and forgotten).

As the records of the Santa Clara Circuit have not been located, we cannot know the extent of Hazen's work at New Almaden from 1863 to 1865: how many he baptized; how many became probationers or full members of the church. From his previous work, though, we can easily imagine his approach to building up the community. The revivals that he mentioned probably involved early morning meetings, before the miners went to work, where a few gathered in the small church, and after fervent prayer, some were moved to approach the front bench. Evening gatherings included men, women and families and probably continued on a nightly basis for perhaps two weeks or even longer, as long as the enthusiasm lasted. The tiny church reverberated with spirited hymn-singing. Hazen no doubt followed Wesley's advice to his preachers — first preach the law, and then forgiveness, enumerating the things that can block a person from experiencing forgiveness and emphasized the gospel of regeneration and hope. Night by night, we can imagine, a few came forward.

In a community starved for diversion the revival period was exciting. In time, without regard to a schedule, the excitement abated and the community returned to its everyday patterns, religious practice resuming its routine of Sunday chapel and class, family devotions and individual meditation. Though many who professed conversion or reconsecration during the revivals probably fell away later, there remained the remnant of a few cataclysmically changed people who became earnest Christians.

During Hazen's tenure, and as evidence of the growth of the Cornish camp and its church, the first child was baptized on Mine Hill, but that baptism may not have had the significance that some of us today would expect. For centuries infant baptism had been controversial in the Christian church, and while defending infant baptism Wesley had introduced a new factor, the importance of conversion. So when Dick Pearce, son of Richard and Louisa Pearce, was dipped in water in the schoolhouse in 1864 (apparently before Hazen's church was completed) he was not fully admitted as a member of the church. We should not imagine the minister tracing the sign of the cross on the infant's forehead or accepting him (as the Anglican Book of Common Prayer puts it), "sealed by the Holy Spirit in Baptism and marked as Christ's own forever." The pastor probably did not refer to the event as a "sacrament," a visible sign of grace, but as an "ordinance," a rather legalistic reference to God's commands in scripture. As Wesley also eliminated the practice of confirmation, full membership in the church for Dick Pearce would have to wait until he became a conscious believer and served a probationary period of six months, and later he could transfer his membership to another church (as he eventually did) with a letter from his pastor.

Hazen was followed on the circuit by other pastors, and they are best remembered for their pioneering efforts in Los Gatos. Dr. William Morrow, a medical man who took up the ministry, is celebrated as the first Methodist minister there. He must have had an impact at New Almaden, too, because he was born in New Jersey (perhaps among the Cornish lead miners) and was remembered for his "Cornish eloquence." Next came the Rev. William Bramwell Priddy, who remembered from his Ohio boyhood how farmers would abandon their plows, wives and daughters would leave the washing, and all would gather to hear the itinerant preacher. When he remembered the Santa Clara Circuit he principally recalled the church at Los Gatos:

> I was appointed to Los Gatos and New Almaden in September 1867. When I went there I found no church property of any kind at Los Gatos. There was a church at New Almaden but no parsonage on the work. I held services under a live oak tree just above the old stone mill [Forbes Mill at Los Gatos] as the weather would permit, but in the meantime I had a church and parsonage in process of erection. I moved into the new parsonage in November. The church was dedicated I think in January 1868 by Dr. Thomas.

Since from surviving letters we know that Priddy was sensitive to nature, we might imagine him riding over the hills from Los Gatos in the Spring, descending the slope into Guadalupe Canyon, fording the stream, and ascending the dusty trail to the mining settlement. He would have noticed the wild flowers, the butter cups, lily-of-the-valley, white and yellow violets, rooster daisies, Jack-in-the-pulpit, the golden poppies, and even the skunk weed. He would have noticed the white oak in flower, the live and scrub oaks, bay trees, buckeye, madrone and manzanita, recognizing in their colors and scents an expression of the God he served. Probably wearing a black coat, and perhaps the bushy brows, wire-framed glasses and the mustache and goatee that characterized him in later years, he would have been comfortable astride a horse, mulling over the words that he would address to the New Almaden society.

With the appointment in 1868 of the Rev. James Corwin, another Methodist pioneer, we see clearly how the circuit had evolved. One Sunday he would preach at eleven o'clock at Los Gatos and ride to the community of Alma at the Santa Cruz summit for a service at four in the afternoon. The next Sunday morning he would preach two sermons near the Guadalupe Mine (another mercury mine) and one on Mine Hill at New Almaden in the evening. Corwin was succeeded by the Rev. Hugh Gibson, who continued the work from 1869 through 1871 (during the first year assisted by F. D. Hodgram). In 1871 the Santa Clara Circuit disappears from the records and is replaced by the "Los Gatos Circuit" and in subsequent years simply by "Los Gatos."

St. Anthony Catholic Church, New Almaden - *The first Christian community at New Almaden was the Roman Catholic, which preceded the Methodist by more than a decade. St. Anthony's (above) was situated in the Spanish-speaking camp. As Spanish Camp had at least double the population of English Camp, the Catholics probably out-numbered the Methodists on Mine Hill by more than two to one. (Laurence Bulmore Collection, Sourisseau Academy, San Jose State University).*

4

The Los Gatos Circuit, 1871 - 1879

You brought them in and planted them
on the mountain of your possession.
Exodus, Chapter 15

Among the population of the American frontier about nine people out of ten were unchurched and in their day the circuit riders rode out to them as John Wesley reiterated 10,000 times, like knights errant, not carrying a shield but a book. Methodism was characterized by such an outward thrust. In California one sees other examples of it in the Methodist ministries to various immigrant groups, the Chinese, Japanese, Germans and Hispanics. While this thrust was always present, and is present in Methodism today, in the era of the Los Gatos Circuit the pastor could at least stable his horse during much of the week. At this time our history acquires a substantial and very Western sense of place, two ridges of foothills running up to the Coast Range, fifty miles south of San Francisco and yet close enough on a summer evening to hear the sunset guns at the Presidio. It also acquires a vivid assortment of individual pastors who could enjoy at least a semi-permanent residence and focus their attention on congregations at Los Gatos and at New Almaden.

Obtaining his appointment from the California Conference of the Methodist Episcopal Church, at the annual meeting of Methodist ministers, superintendents and usually a bishop, the Rev. A. C. Hazzard was the first pastor appointed to the Los Gatos Circuit. Hazzard reported forty-four communicants, two churches (Los Gatos and New Almaden) valued at $1,500, and the Los Gatos parsonage valued at $500. During Hazzard's tenure James Randol, newly arrived from New York, was settling in as the mine's general manager and was discovering that there were already at least sixty Cornish living on Mine Hill. Randol admired their work ethic andl advertised for more like them in the newspapers of Nevada County, California and Cornwall. By 1880 the population of "English Town" (the Quicksilver Mining Company's name for what the residents called "Cornish camp" or "English camp") increased to several hundred and changed from a population dominated by single men to one of predominantly families and children.

Much of this happened during the Rev. William Gafney's time on the Los Gatos circuit, returning to the area after having previously served there as a preacher in training. He was one of the most influential pastors to take charge, though perhaps the least likely to succeed. Extremely reticent, almost painfully diffident, Gafney was a pioneer of California Methodism, a class leader beginning in 1851 at a church on Powell Street in San Francisco. A woman in his class reported, "Brother Gafney has a call to the ministry and is resisting it." Since the Methodists sorely needed pastors at that time, Gafney was not allowed to resist for long, yet that painful diffidence stayed with him and probably condemned him to a career of impoverished appointments. In 1858 he traveled the Santa Clara Circuit for $487 per year at a time when the best appointments paid about $1500. During his years on the Los Gatos Circuit (1872-75) he earned only about $800 annually (earnings comparable to those of an experienced miner). He was never a popular preacher but what tactful colleagues called "a useful one." The faithful at Los Gatos and New Almaden found him solemn and even austere, but with a "warm heart beating beneath a cold exterior."

We see how effective Gafney was when he momentarily threw off his reserve to give, like the good slave in the parable of the talents, an account of his three years on the circuit. He provided the unique spelling of "Guadalupe" in this 1875 letter to the editor of the California *Christian Advocate* (the Methodist newspaper).

Los Gatos Circuit

Mr. Editor:—As I am about to close my third year at this place, perhaps a brief account of the work may be proper.

The circuit embraces Los Gatos, the New Almaden and Guadaloupe quicksilver mines. Through the instrumentality of Thomas A. Mitchell and Joseph S. Richards, two worthy local preachers (the latter of whom was taken away by death on the 27th of last June, which resulted from severe cold — taken by coming out of a very hot place in the mine into the cold night air), religious services were commenced early last spring at the Guadaloupe mine, resulting in the organization of a Sunday-school, and the formal organization of a class of Church members last April, which now numbers twelve. They have their regular weekly prayer and class meetings; and, with the aid of the pastor once in four weeks, and local brethren of the circuit, they have preaching every Sabbath evening.

During my pastoral term, there have been forty-two children and one adult baptized; and forty-two persons received into the Church on probation; one of whom died, three were dropped, six moved away before their probation expired, ten are received in full membership, and twenty-two still on probation; most of whom were brought in during the revival meetings, which were held with the aid of brethren and sisters from San Jose. Forty persons have been received into the church by letter and by recognition. Within the last two years the full membership of the circuit has just probaabout doubled, and within the last year it has increased from forty to sixty-five. Nearly all the increase has been at Almaden and Guadaloupe.

My salary is all provided for, and, by the blessing of Divine grace, I will leave the charge, as a whole, in a prosperous condition.

Wm. Gafney.

During the "Los Gatos" period, before New Almaden became a separate station, Gafney and his successors brought a total of seventy-two new members into the church. Many of them became leaders or were members of leading families on Mine Hill, including Susan Bunney, Richard Faull, William Geach, Martha Jane Geach, Richard and Louisa Pearce, Samuel Henwood, John and Susanna Tregonning, Charles James and Louisa Varcoe. Of the forty-two children Gafney baptized on the Los Gatos Circuit at least eighteen lived on the hill. In 1876 his immediate successor, the Rev. Hopkins, brought a class of ten new members into the church, including Mary Heathorne, Samuel Argall, Matthew Willoughby, Constance Nichols, and my ancestor William John Hicks, the only one of four Hicks brothers from Redruth, Cornwall, to have his name recorded in the church ledger. No doubt the pinnacle of the year that the Rev. R. W. Williamson spent on the hill was the day in July 1879 when he received fourteen into the church, including Alfred Tregonning and William Dunstan. Following him was the Rev. Jesse Smith, the last to have responsibility for both Los Gatos and New Almaden, who conducted a well-publicized camp meeting in the vicinity of the mine.

In September 1879 New Almaden appears in the Methodist rolls for the first time as a separate charge, a congregation strong enough to support its own pastor. The first pastor assigned, the Rev. George W. Beatty, served at New Almaden until 1881.

5

Church Building, 1875 - 1885

The sparrow has found her house
and the swallow a nest where she may lay her young
by the side of your altars, O Lord of hosts . . . .
Psalm 84

During Gafney's tenure a delegation of miners called on the general manager of the Quicksilver Mining Company to seek support for building a new and larger Methodist Church on Mine Hill. We might call them a "delegation of husbands." It was the women on the hill who saw that a proper church would help to make the camp a better place for families and they pushed the men forward. Randol, who recognized the wisdom of the proposal and was capable of calculating that a family camp would give him a stable work force, pledged that the company would match the funds raised by the employees for the building of a church.

What we know about the various church buildings erected on the hill is sketchy as only one of them survived into the twentieth century. We know that the churches stood on Church Hill, a spur of Mine Hill, and that the Cornish camp lay in the saddle between the two heights. The first of the churches built by the company and community was dedicated on, of course, a rainy Easter Sunday, 1875. Even on such an important occasion a simple service would have featured singing, extemporaneous prayer and preaching. The occasion was marked by having a guest preacher, the Rev. Charles V. Anthony, an impressive preacher and later the historian of California Methodism, who probably preached in the conventional long black coat.

Were we able to walk into that church today we would probably be impressed by its simple sanctity, the clean-swept wooden floor, the redwood joist and beams. With no surviving photographs to guide us we can safely presume that the pulpit was prominent and that the church was not decorated, except perhaps for two candles on an altar, and if there was also a cross some of the old Cornish may have grumbled, "Idolatry." There were benches in front for the choir and perhaps the church leaders, so they could set an example. Oil lamps probably provided light on dark days, while on bright ones sunlight angled in through the tall, clear

The church re-built after the 1884 fire - *The last and best Methodist church building included a basement for classes and lodge meetings. A steep staircase led up to the nave with its tall, arched windows and high ceiling. "Were we able to walk into that church today we would probably be impressed by its simple sanctity . . . ."(New Almaden Museum).*

windows and through an occasional chink in the redwood paneling. On that Easter day or any day, sitting in the stillness of the wooden pews, one would have heard the wind, or at least a faint breeze, along the eaves and about the steeple.

The worship on that Easter was indicative of the services throughout the era of the New Almaden church. Individual pastors had wide prerogatives, though, so over the years services would not have been uniform. The morning services probably would have included an opening hymn that everyone sang while seated, prayer (customarily kneeling), the reading of a lesson (perhaps an entire chapter) from the Old Testament of the Bible and one from the New, preaching, the Lord's Prayer, more hymns and a benediction. An evening service would have included perhaps a single lesson, hymns and preaching.

Though the Wesleys had been high church Anglicans who took communion twice a week, their preferences were jettisoned in the mid-Atlantic. During the time of our history American Methodism was usually non-liturgical and non-sacramental, its extemporized services emphasizing the importance of personal faith. The Lord's Supper, as it was called, would have been observed perhaps quarterly, and often these occasions would coincide with a visit from the Presiding Elder, who superintended the San Francisco District, all the Methodist churches from San Francisco to Monterey. Some of these elders were outstanding leaders, missionaries to California, and heroes of the movement, such as George Clifford, Joseph Wythe, Wesley Dennett, H. B. Heacock and Henry Bland. Most of them had earned doctorates in divinity, and as they worked on a broad scale, their careers were marked by industry and vision.

Worship services continued in that 1875 church for less than a year. Sometime during the first winter, after Gafney left and the Rev. Hopkins took charge, a fierce gale blew the church down. A second more substantial structure, that included a full basement, replaced it. Despite having to rebuild, these were good years for the Mine Hill church and they justified, in the spirit of St. Paul's letters, a bit of boasting. When the Rev. Beatty wrote a report to the California *Christian Advocate*, giving a glimpse of the church, its furnishings, functions and activities, he was in part responding to a recent series of articles that had appeared decrying debt. He also explained (consistent with Methodism's outward thrust) that regular Methodist services had begun at The Hacienda, the community below Mine Hill where the mine manager and executives lived.

New Almaden, Sept. 7, 1880

Eleven person united with the church on the 29th and 31st of Aug. Three on probation, one by letter and seven from probation. "Praise God from whom all blessings flow!" As freedom from church debt seems to be the special cause of praise this year, we can ask all to unite with us on that basis also. The trustee's report now before me shows: Debt from last year, $10.40; Organ, $111.75; Improvements, $159.85; A total of $282.00 all paid except $18.50 and that provided for in the near future. Adding to this the Sunday-school expenses for the year all paid, $85.00, collections taken, $25.00; salary paid, $650.00; and we have the sum of $1024.50 from a place which has been one of four appointments to pay $920. The above is the Hill report. The Hacienda has done nobly, $258, from a point where a Sabbath-school has never before been organized nor regular services held. We could wish more of the above was "Pastor's support," yet we rejoice to see a new organ and new Sunday-school song books at each point. If we do not return to reap, some good brother will enter upon our labors. The Hill Sabbath-school has an average enrollment of 136 and an average attendance of 111. The Hacienda numbers 31 with an average attendance of 29. Better still, 95 per cent of the Hacienda school remain to preaching and 75 per cent of the Hill school return to evening service. Best of all the financial statements. The pastor's salary is paid *monthly* in *advance*. We almost lost our equilibrium when paid a month's salary the first week of our pastorate. How soon we become accustomed to any treatment! These monthly ordeals are now passed without a tremor, in fact, we rather enjoy them.

Pastor

The church built on the brow of the high hill, exposed to the south, bore little resemblance to any Methodist chapel that the inhabitants of the Cornish camp had seen back home. As a rule Methodist chapels in Cornwall were (and are today) architecturally plain, often square, unadorned, utilitarian buildings, located on streets or roads near the cottages of working people and not on prominent points of land. They stand as a rebuke to the pretensions of the vaulted and steepled Anglican churches that bear the names of the old Cornish saints and the inscriptions of land-owning families and wealthy mining adventurers. The church built on Mine Hill, rather than resembling the ones back home, had a decidedly American style, looking like something borrowed from Congregational New England. The photographs that survive show a white picket fence surrounding a white board church with arched windows and a high, symmetrical steeple that rises to one side, rather than from the center of the church.

The course of its history was never easy, and the church was damaged by winds almost every winter. Then a worse disaster — on the night of 5 September 1884 the church burnt to the ground. "While over to Oldham [a nearby ranch] we were called to the door," an eighteen year old witness, Charles Schneider, noted in his journal. "We stepped on to the porch where we saw that the church at upper Almaden was on fire. It was a very pretty sight."

Not so pretty to those on the scene, who were only able to save the organ and a few pews, water being scarce on the hill. One of those was Captain James Harry, a native of Breage, Cornwall, who supervised 350 men at the quicksilver mine. He gave a brief history (His account overlooks the little church built by the Rev. Hazen).

Q. What do you know about the Building of the church here and how it came to be built, and the history of the church?

A. I do not exactly remember the date that the first church was built, but the first church was built one-story, built by subscriptions here at the mine. The first time Mr. Randol gave $250 and the company $250; the first winter the church blew down. Mr. Randol said if we wanted a good church to go on and take up our subscriptions and that whatever we subscribed in the community that he would double it; that he would give as much as all the rest; the whole amount that we had from Mr. Randol and the company that time was $848; afterwards the church was again destroyed by fire: that was, I think, in 1884, and again we had to appeal to Mr. Randol, and again he gave from the company $500, and his own personal subscription was $355, and the balance of the money was raised by subscription from the people working on the Quicksilver Mining Company's grant; that church cost $3,450. That is the present church; Mr. Randol has subscribed towards the Protestant church on the Hill $2,203 since he has been here.

Q. How many people will that church accommodate?

A. About 250 or 300.

Q. How is it generally filled at religious services?

A. Filled to the fullest capacity. In fact our pastor is talking about enlarging; the Sunday school is held there Sunday afternoons. We have a fine Sunday school with an average attendance of 165 to 170; those are the children of the people who work for the company; the Good Templars' Lodge meets in the basement story, and the Miners' Benevolent Society.

While the Quicksilver Mining Company and general manager made conspicuous contributions to the church, so did the California Conference. At its annual meeting in Pacific Grove, September 1884, the ministers addressed the case of New Almaden through a series of motions:

New Almaden Church.—W. Dennett [presiding elder] presented the following, and it was adopted:

WHEREAS, We have no deed for the church lot at New Almaden and can secure none, the mining company owning all the property and simply charging a nominal rent of one dollar per year, and,

WHEREAS, At the dedication the property was delivered over to the Trustees (duly elected) free of debt, and,

WHEREAS, The church members are poor day laborers with two or three exceptions, and,

WHEREAS, The church building has been lately burned, nothing being saved but the seats and organ; and,

WHEREAS, There was no insurance on the property, therefore,

RESOLVED, That a committee of five be appointed to inquire into the case and report what steps, if any, should be taken in the premises, and report to the Conference.

The committee recommended that the Church Extension Board contribute $500 to the rebuilding of the New Almaden church, provided the trustees buy insurance, a policy payable to the board. In the final rebuilding the church was moved into the lee of Mine Hill where violent storms could no longer cause substantial damage.

James Butterworth Randol - General manager, 1870 - 92.
(New Almaden Museum)

6

Church Pastors

O Lord, you are my portion and my cup;
it is you who uphold my lot.
Psalm 16

Reality, a poet tells us, is the best dream we will ever know. If we consider the history of this church as a dream of the past that plays in our minds today, a dream illumined by imagination and prescribed by fact, we need numinous characters that are large enough to fill the landscape of a dream. Fact supplies these in the stories of the church pastors who, as in any church, compose so much of its history. The courage, fortitude and commitment of these men, who lived their lives under rustic and sometimes harrowing conditions, make them symbolic actors, heroes both in legend and in truth.

In the nineteenth century the isolation of people of learning or sensibility was commonplace, and one reads of it in England in the novels of Thomas Hardy and in the American West in the story of many frontier doctors, lawyers and engineers. The ministers at New Almaden were just such people as these, well-educated men for their day, fully capable of feeling the harshness of their surroundings. In their educational backgrounds, though, there was little uniformity. Among the better educated, The Rev. Thomas Hopkins had earned a Master's degree at Genesee College (later Syracuse University). Among those with less education, the Rev. Charles Grey Milne scarcely had any formal training beyond a country school, but was reputed to have a thorough self-education, and in the parlance of the day "he wrested out of hardships the fine gold of a resplendent character." Others had graduated or at least attended various Wesleyan colleges and seminaries, including the Rev. Priddy, who worked as a miner to earn his tuition to the College of the Pacific in San Jose (now the University of the Pacific, Stockton). Some, such as the Rev. Marion Willis, had experience as school masters. They all continued their learning after their ordinations, reading in the saddle as Wesley had done.

One of their band, Henry Clark Benson, doctor of divinity and student by instinct, was the most learned man ever to inhabit Mine Hill.

Benson taught in a country school for eight years to pay his way through Indiana Wesleyan University. As a minister he taught among the Choctaws in Arkansas and wrote a book about his experiences. Proficient in Latin, Greek and Hebrew, he later became a professor at his alma mater. He transferred to California, served at various stations and then edited Methodist newspapers in Portland and San Francisco for sixteen years. After resigning his editorship he came to New Almaden (1888 - 90), far removed from the varied life that he had known in the cities. It may have been about this time that he was studying medicine for, ever the student, he eventually earned a medical degree. After leaving New Almaden he became president of the College of the Pacific. A handsome man with an ascetic, clean-shaven face, Benson was a natural leader when the ministers met at the Conference each year. At the meetings, a colleague said, "He usually voted with the majority not because he was a follower, but because others followed him."

All of the ministers had rich experiences before they arrived at New Almaden and those included the most trying kind. At least three of them served in the Civil War, including Thomas Hopkins, who fought with the 107th New York Volunteer in Sherman's bloodiest campaigns. Beatty enlisted as a teenager in the Union army; and Joseph R. Wolfe rose to the rank of captain with the 107th Illinois. Wolfe, who had a Lincolnesque education of borrowed books and apprenticeships, later practiced law and ran for office.

All of them had seen considerable service in California, and having ridden circuits from the southern Sierra to the Oregon border, they knew the state and its people well. To give but one example, the Rev. Dr. William Smith Urmy (like Benson, a doctor of divinity) was aging by the time he came to New Almaden in 1905-06. He began his ministry in Coloma, where gold was discovered, and later served the Sonora and Columbia circuit with responsibility for all of Tuolumne County. When serving a circuit in Amador County he got lost and wandered into the town of Sutter Creek where, on a moment's notice, a congregation gathered in the school house to hear the first sermon ever delivered there. His career spanned forty-three years and many pastorates.

Many of the pastors had some of the carpentry skills that Christianity has always valued and extensive experience building churches. Hopkins said of himself, "During my ministry I have built four churches and four parsonages and have tried to fight a good fight and do a good work, but it has never equaled my desires." They all could have said that. John W.

38

Edward Adams Hazen   *H. C. Benson, DD.*

J. W. Buxton   *C. V. Anthony*

(Archives, United Methodist Church, Berkeley & Stockton)

39

Bryant from Wisconsin, erected churches at Crescent City, Lodi, Woodland and Hollister and parsonages at Santa Cruz and Salinas. He held 17 pastorates and saw "more than a thousand souls added to the church."

Two of the ministers had experience in the desert of Nevada before they came to New Almaden. When the Rev. Francis Marion Willis took up the ministry in 1862, he connected with the Nevada Conference and served Honey Lake Circuit, American and Indian Valley, Walker River, Bishop, Independence, and Antelope. His physical strength (not to mention religious convictions) enabled him to establish churches and erect buildings with his own hands. A colleague said, "He made the desert to blossom as the rose."

Willis' friend in Nevada, and later his successor at New Almaden, the Rev. J. L. Trefren, founded an unique venture in the history of the church — "The Methodist Mining Company." Trefren was stationed in Austin, a boom town with daily murders, which was described by a medical doctor in a letter dated 1863:

> . . . no church or place of innocent amusement here. The Society here is perhaps the most loose and rough that were ever collected at any one point since Noah's time. It averages from one to three men every day shot. The most reckless and wicked men I have ever come in contact with, but I find plenty of good, honest and pleasant men.

With his white hair and beard, boyish, cherub-like face and shiny dark eyes, Trefren hardly appeared suitable for such a place, and yet perhaps by being pure with the pure and wily with the crooked he mastered the situation. In an effort to raise money for the Methodist Church, he asked for blocks of stock in the various mines and organized a holding company, The Methodist Mining Company. He went to his native New Hampshire where he sold $350,000 of the company's securities, and by agreement with the mining companies, kept ten per cent of all he sold. With that he built a large brick church and parsonage and began to change the tenor of Austin. The miracle in this story is that the mines paid so well that the Yankee investors suffered no losses, or at least that's the way it has been told. When Trefren came to Mine Hill his surname — by "Tre," "Pol" and "Pen," you shall know a Cornishman — would have earned him a kinsman's welcome.

As personalities these pastors contributed generously to the life on Mine Hill and some of them were remembered for their sense of presence. The Rev. Hopkins, with a tuft of white hair at the peak of his broad forehead, deep-set, dark eyes, mustache and clerical collar, was one of those best remembered:

> Brother Hopkins dealt with people personally, and not professionally. There was a kindliness in his tones, a sincerity in his inquiries, a magnetic genuinesss in his handclasp, and, withal, that subtle something which drew people to him and convinced them of his unselfish devotion to their interests. In many, many homes he was a part of the family life. In sorrow he was there to comfort, not merely as a minister, but as one who could weep in truest sympathy. Every festal gathering he attended was sanctified by his presence.

One imagines that the Rev. William J. Peters had a special relationship with the New Almaden congregation because, coming from Cornwall himself, he could speak to them of home. Like them, too, he had seen a fair portion of the world, having preached in Methodist Churches on three continents. Peters was born in 1856 in the village of Portscatho, on Cornwall's tranquil southern coast. No one recorded what took him to South America (copper mining most likely), but there he became a lay preacher. Later he returned to Cornwall where he continued preaching for another eight years. About 1884 he came out to Yuba City, California, where two of his sisters lived, and there he became a Methodist minister on trial. He served in Roseville, Fort Jones, Florin and Point Arena before coming to New Almaden (1895-98) for three years, the maximum time then allowed by the Conference. During his tenure he had 77 probationers in classes and he received 27 of them into full membership.

After leaving New Almaden some of the younger ministers went on to distinguished careers, especially the Rev. George W. Beatty, who made a name in Santa Clara County where he was farsighted and resourceful in his charges. After his New Almaden years he became the first pastor of the new Centella Church in San Jose, which held its first services in a former saloon at the gore of First and Market Streets. From 1887-90 he took charge of Los Gatos, putting his energy behind the construction of a new church building, resuscitating the Methodist society in Saratoga and organizing a new church in Campbell. A colleague described him as "radiant, cheerful, hopeful, sincere, transparent and companionable," and even after one hundred years we can discern those qualities in his photograph, in his radiant expression, large, mobile eyes, wavy dark hair, and trimmed goatee.

If any one wonders about the commitment of these men to the gospel they preached, one needs only hear how their careers ended. When Gafney, aging and feeble, was told that he must retire from the active ministry he wept. He lived on for several years, assisting in churches in Sonoma County until the end. On a sunny May morning he called out to his wife, "Good bye! I'm happy! Hallelujah!," and he died. Too infirm in his last days to attend the Annual Conference, Milne sent a letter saying, "I rejoice that ever God counted me worthy to be in the ministry." Partially paralyzed and feeling the life leaving him, Dr. Morrow wanted a visiting minister to hear his final testimony:

> He was scarcely able to articulate intelligibly, even in a whisper; and yet, he seemed anxious to magnify God's saving grace. Said he, "The gospel which I have preached saves. . . . There is a revelation in the heart that is only known by experience," he said.

He died in San Jose on April 3, 1903. In a letter at the end of his life Hopkins wrote, "The dear Lord knows all about it and he will do better by us all than we deserve."

7

Madonnas of the Trail:
Pastors' Wives

My soul magnifies the Lord
and my spirit rejoices in God my Savior.
Luke, Chapter 1

When the church descendants gathered at New Almaden on that rainy day in 1995, they heard Janet Engle, historian of the Los Gatos First United Methodist Church, talk about women of the church. She took her theme from a series of female statues that the National Old Trails Associations and the Daughters of the American Revolution dedicated years ago to mark the Westward trails. "Each statue depicts a pioneer woman in sunbonnet, flowing skirt and boots, walking, carrying a small child and with another child tugging at her skirt," Engle said. On each an inscription reads, "Madonna of the Trail — memorial to the Pioneer Mothers of the Covered Wagon Days." "Pastors wives," Engle continued, "joined their husbands as yokemates to the gospel. They were the Methodist Madonnas of the itinerant trail."

Like other women in California, the pastors' wives either knew the hardships of crossing the prairie or the dangers of ocean passage and malarial swamps. Like other women, they probably had been reluctant to make the journey in the first place, regretting the rending of families and communities. On the trail, where they suffered physical hardships alongside the men, their privacy and sanitary requirements (not to mention pregnancies) were little considered and they suffered great loneliness. Those who came West as children and who later married ministers — such as Emma Willis and Agnes Bryant — may have not fully recognized the dangers of the journey and may have even seen the fun of it. Those who came as grown women faced the dangers squarely and had their faith tested along the way.

Perhaps none of the wives who came to New Almaden knew the prairie as did Armenda Luella Taylor. She was born in Illinois in 1859 and as a child moved with her family to Missouri. When she was fourteen the family pressed on to Kansas where in nomadic fashion her father pitched a tent on the prairie. Before he could finish building a house, he perished in a Kansas blizzard. A year later, at fifteen, she married Theodore Taylor and saw him fail to eke a living from the soil. The following year she and her husband walked beside their ox-drawn wagon, trekking across the plains, climbing and descending the mountains. "The lines for this devoted couple never fell in easy places," a friend wrote. "They early knew pioneer hardships."

Women who came by sea knew hardships, too. Lizzie Hazen came to California by the Isthmus of Panama and arrived in San Francisco in December 1852 suffering from yellow fever. It was one of the wettest winters on record and rained constantly. After a week she and the Rev. Hazen took a steamer to Alviso, where they boarded a six-horse stage to San Jose, eight miles away. In the first mile the stage mired in the mud, forcing them to horseback. The horse on which Mrs. Hazen rode with the stage driver lurched in the mud, throwing them both — and this was Christmas day! The Hazens were never adequately provided for through a series of appointments in northern California and more than once, when food ran low, they almost literally lived on prayer. In time Mrs. Hazen was worn out and her health failed. Her husband considered giving up the ministry, but instead he built a house in Santa Clara, situated his wife there, and rode the Santa Clara Circuit. He served New Almaden and the other stations, visiting his wife and family as his schedule allowed.

One of the ministers' wives, Mrs. W. J. Peters, had crossed an ocean as well as a continent, and having come from ancestral Cornwall she had the most in common with the women on Mine Hill. At age 89, retired in Pacific Grove, she appended a few lines about herself to her husband's story.

> So all I can add to it is that my husband came out from England about a year before I came, a promise from me that I would follow him, so with the "consent" of my dear parents, I came and met my friends in Yuba City, two of his sisters with him. So we were married by Rev. Woodward who was the Pastor at Marysville, not far from us. Mr. Peters was preaching there in "Yuba City." He was about seven or eight years older than myself. From there later on we were sent to Roseville & remained there three years. At that time it meant that three years was the limit—we were very happy.

When she arrived at Mine Hill in 1895 she could have compared her story with those of other women — they probably knew people in common back home.

By the mid-nineteenth century the Methodist church and its congregations expected the ministers' wife to have education and a variety of specialized skills that were unique to her situation, practically a recognized vocation. Like the pastors at New Almaden, many of the pastors' wives were well acquainted with classrooms. Mrs. Lucy M. Gaffney taught school in Santa Cruz before her marriage; Juletta Coil Wolfe attended the State Normal College in Bloomington, Illinois. Mrs. W. S. Urmy (then Miss Eliza Bradford Pettis) graduated from a "high-grade seminary" in her native Somerset, Massachusetts, and taught in the public schools for perhaps fifteen years before coming to California.

In their families the pastors' wives bore primary responsibility for child rearing. They could not count on their husbands who, preoccupied with reading and preaching, attending to classes, visiting the sick, and traveling, might become strangers to the family. The wives were responsible for seeing their children properly schooled. They raised their broods in knowledge that the community had higher expectation for the behavior of the minister's children than for other children. This must have weighed especially on those with the largest families, such as Mrs. Willis with nine children; Mrs. Benson, five sons and four daughters; and Mrs. Taylor, four sons.

The ministers' wives at New Almaden probably had access to the special manuals published at mid century for their sakes, such as the Rev. Herrick M. Eaton's *The Itinerant's Wife: Her Qualifications, Duties, Trials, and Rewards.* Eaton wrote a sympathetic and often wise commentary that offered the sage advice that "the itinerant's wife should love the itinerancy." No doubt the women were as committed to the work as were their husbands, and without the encouragement and prayerful support of their wives, many preachers would have given up.

No words of advice, though, could spare the pastors' wives from the depressing recurrence of packing up, parting from friends, severing ties and moving every one to three years as the itinerant scheme required. One wife recalled:

> In old times husbands went where all the tribes do gather, not knowing what would befall them there. And wives waited for the reading of the appointments while getting ready to move . . . Dark side of itinerant life this moving is! Yet tired feet and aching hearts never allow a dark side where love and loyalty hold sway.

Some of these women moved as many as twenty times during their husbands' careers, and the repetition made it no easier to say good bye.

Emma Margaret Steele Willis

The Rev. Francis Marion Willis

(Russell Pearce Collection)

The three-year limit held until near the turn of the century, and then increased to five, though no pastoral family stayed that long at New Almaden.

The pastors' wives set a tone for their neighbors not only of morality, but of piety and civility. By living their faith, they reasserted the patterns of domestic and social life that people had left behind when they traveled West. New Almaden remembered the pastors' wives as saints. The report on Mrs. Trefren was typical: she "loved humanity, sympathized with all kinds of sorrow, prized the Church, and with a burning desire to honor her Savior bent all her consecrated energies to his cause." "Her name and memory," the Conference minutes tell us, "are as precious ointment." Matilda Benson "was as one who knew God face to face and what she thus learned, she gave to others." Armenda Taylor's hand was "a touch of tenderness and strength to many who needed Christ-like friendship; while her caress of kindness eased the way of numbers of weary pilgrims passing through the valley of the shadow of death." Juletta Wolfe, though quiet, retiring and undemonstrative, was remembered as a woman whose strong character supported her husband. One writer especially remembered Hester Buxton for her influence on him when he was growing up on Mine Hill.

> Mrs. Buxton will be best remembered by her friends for her unfailing fidelity to her husband and the work of the church to which they gave their devotion and love in unstinted measure. It was in the little church on the mountain at New Almaden that the writer came as a boy to know this good woman and to appreciate her Christ-like character. Always cheerful, buoyant of spirit, radiating that light of Christian love and kindness by which she won the hearts of both old and young. Who shall measure the influence of such a life lived in such simplicity and complete abandon to the things of the spirit? Truly the lives of many were made sweeter by her presence and that influence shall never cease.

In a few cases, reflecting the changing roles of women, ministers' wives became leaders in the community and assistants to the ordained men. Mary Gough played such a part and with a vigor that caused her husband to often say, "Dear wife, put on the brakes." Years of exertion cost Mrs. Gough her health, which failed while her husband was serving at New Almaden. Emma Margaret Steele Willis turned the wives' share of her husband's work into something of a co-pastorate. "Her services were in continuous request as an advocate of religious and the temperance causes," a contemporary tells us. "Her voice was often heard in Sunday School Conventions and in public assemblies where a larger field for woman's work was discussed. Often she took the Pastor's place in neighboring appointments."

Most of the wives remained in the church as widows, often singing in choirs and teaching Bible classes. Once widowed, most relied on the meager pension provided by the Conference, as did Lucy M. Gafney. The Conference records tell us that "she bore uncomplainingly the burdens of her widowhood and poverty, but she was ever true in word and deed to her divine Master." In 1891 (when the average salary of a pastor was $1200) she received $250 from the Conference. In subsequent years pensions increased, especially thanks to the Rev. J. H. Wythe, Jr. Wythe served at New Almaden in 1881-82, but more importantly for the widows, he later served as the pension fund's principal agent and in that role displayed an uncommon business acumen.

The life of the itinerant preacher's wife was trying, yet by all we know every pastor's wife who came to New Almaden was obedient and loyal to her special calling. With what thoughts and emotions, we might wonder, did they join their voices in the singing of this popular Methodist hymn?

> In hope of that immortal crown,
> I now the cross sustain,
> And gladly wander up and down,
> And smile at toil and pain,
>
> I suffer on, my threescore years,
> Till my Deliverer come,
> To wipe away his servant's tears,
> And take his exile home.

8

"The Surest Steps Out of the Mine":
Lay Preachers

He lifted me out of the desolate pit,
out of the mire and clay;
he set my feet upon a high cliff
and made my footing sure.
Psalm 40

At Methodist Church Day I spoke briefly on the significant role that nineteenth century Methodism gave to lay people in the functions of the church. The Methodist movement gathered working people, such as the miners and their families at New Almaden, and from the assemblage it encouraged the development of leaders, people who could read, think and speak for themselves and who could help to direct their community. Methodism's emphasis on the reformation of the individual promoted self-improvement, and the church gave opportunity and encouragement to those who were able to lead.

First among these were the "local preachers." As Methodism developed in Britain and America, local preachers were licensed to serve in a particular place under the supervision of the pastor. Lay people began taking a turn in the pulpit in the time of John Wesley, an Anglican priest who guarded the prerogatives of the ordained minister, but who came to rely more and more, reluctantly at first, but later cheerfully, on preachers who came from the ranks of working people. He chose them for their personal knowledge of salvation, and set them on a course of reading, expecting them to spend five hours a day in study. Opportunity arose for local preachers at New Almaden where there was Sabbath preaching in the morning and evening both on the hill and at The Hacienda. Selected laymen preached on Sundays, and during the rest of the week retained their jobs as engine operators, muckers, or tribute miners. Unlike the ordained ministers, most of whom had at least a semblance of university training, the local preachers were primarily self-educated.

"Never license a local preacher," advised the Methodist newspaper, "who does not have such a burning zeal for the cause of Christ as to make him feel, 'Woe is me if I preach not the Gospel.'" This was the zeal that prompted all the local preachers on Mine Hill. We have few written accounts of the ministry of these preachers and know little beyond the fact that their preaching helped the church to remain close to the immediate concerns of the people. We know a little of the work of John Harris, a practical miner who left England in the 1850s and worked in Pennsylvania and Virginia before coming to California, and his of friend Thomas Vivian, also from Cornwall.

> These faithful local preachers [their pastor reported] dispense the word of life from the pulpit, and from house to house, in the absence of the regular pastor. They also sustain the prayer meetings and Sunday school.

We know from their pastor's report (quoted above) that Thomas A. Mitchell and Joseph S. Richards became local preachers and helped him to extend Methodism to the Guadalupe Mine and The Hacienda. We have evidence that William Stiles, a furnace foreman, and John Tregoning, Thomas H. Morcum and Joseph Richard, all miners, took their turns in the pulpit and led prayers in the 1870s; and we have the names of several others as listed in the appendix. Most were appointed for a year or two and not renewed, presumably because they were not effective preachers, did not care for the assignment, or exhausted themselves in the work.

These men were like the famous men in scriptures who were once the lights of their generation but whose names are now forgotten, or all but forgotten. Just as did some of the Cornish mining captains who in their times became superintendent of the mine — Richard Pearce, James Harry and John Drew — the local preachers demonstrated to the Cornish camp that leadership did not come only from the university-trained engineers who surveyed the mine or from La Casa Grande of the wealthy mine manager. Scholarship was not the exclusive prerogative of the pastor or the school master. Leadership arose, too, from within their ranks of working people and everyone (and everyone's child) had an opportunity to learn. A good example was the local preacher Edwin P. Willoughby, whose typical story included atypical success. He had entered the mines in Cornwall at age nine and had come to America at eighteen. In 1885 he installed the skip road at the Santa Isabel shaft on Mine Hill. As a result of skill, aptitude and study he became an assistant to Professor S. B. Christy of the College of Mining and Metallurgy at the University of California, Berkeley and later crowned his career by becoming superintendent of the Soledad Mine in Mexico.

The most prominent local preacher was another miner, and the descendant of miners, Henry Tregoning. He was born 12 November 1849 to Cornish parents, John and Susannah Tregoning. He saw the light of day in Wales, where his father probably had found work in copper smelting, and was raised in Cornwall, near Par where his siblings were born. He emigrated to America at the age of twenty-three and came to New Almaden. He was first appointed a local preacher in 1872 and three years later he married Lucy Gray, daughter of Captain William Gray, superintendent of the mine, the Rev. Gafney presiding at the wedding.

"By his modest and appreciative spirit," said a friend, "Tregoning was always a learner." He needed an insatiable appetite for learning to keep up with the course of study prescribed in 1880 by the Methodist Episcopal Church. While taking his turn in the pulpit perhaps fifty times a year, he was also working through the "Course of Study of Local Preachers," preparing himself for examinations in the common branches of a liberal education as well as knowledge of the Bible and church doctrines. The reading lists included the following:

First year: *Outlines of Bible History*, by Hurst; *Catechism of the Methodist Church*, No. 3; *Christian Theology* (introduction and book 1) by Wakefield; *Discipline of the Methodist Episcopal Church* (1880 edition); *Life of Wesley*, by Watson; *One Hundred Years of Methodism*, by Simpson

Second year: *The Bible: Doctrines; Christian Theology* (books II & III); *Christian Baptism*, by Merrill; *Outlines of Church History*, by Hurst; *History of the United States*, by Ridpath; *Compendium of Methodism*, by Porter

Third year: *The Bible: Sacraments; Christian Theology* (books IV & V); *Plain Account of Christian Perfection*, by John Wesley; *Rhetoric*, by Haven; *Wesley's Sermons* (volume 1); *Introduction to the Gospel Records*, by Nast; *Era of the Protestant Reformation*, by Seebohn

Fourth year: *Christian Theology* (books VI & VII); *Logic* (Science Primer Edition) by Jevons; *History of Methodism*, by Porter; *Wesley's Sermons* (volume 2); review of the previous three years.

No doubt Tregoning referred often to an additional volume on the list, Porter's *Hints to Self Educated Ministers.* His commitment to study probably explains why Tregoning ceased to work as a miner and became a night watchman for the Quicksilver Mining Company. By lamplight he must have kept watch over his books.

During his many years on Mine Hill there was never a time when Tregoning was not a leader in the church. Along with preaching he also led classes, served in various church offices and was Superintendent of the Sunday School. Beyond New Almaden he held other responsible positions. At a time when the laity were demanding a greater role in governing the church, he was elected president of the Lay Association of the California Annual Conference of the Methodist Episcopal Church in 1896. Under his leadership the association passed a resolution supporting women's suffrage. Tregoning supported the anti-saloon movement and depreciated the association's tendency to put ordained ministers on the program rather than lay people. He was also a leader of the Order of the Sons of St. George, a fraternal organization for the British-born that met at New Almaden as the General Gordon Chapter, named for the hero of the British Empire and martyr of Khartoum.

Tregoning never left his lay ministry though he left New Almaden in 1888 and lived in Grass Valley for a year, where he probably worked in mining. From there he moved to the College Park district of San Jose, near the College of the Pacific, where at last his ministry led him up from the mine. He continued as a local preacher at the College Park Methodist Church and was affiliated with the College of Pacific in what a newspaper called a "humble capacity." He died 21 April 1906, age fifty-six, just three days after the great earthquake, having lived the short life of one whose lungs were permanently damaged underground. At Tregoning's funeral Professor Cross of the college called him a good preacher and said that, "If he had the advantage of a college education his talents would surely have given him great prominence in the world."

Along with his remarkable talents, Tregoning must have been blessed with humility. All the Cornish on Mine Hill were trying to get ahead, trying to help their children to a better life than they had known, which is why they came to America. Yet the Cornish were known in their homeland and abroad for despising anyone who rose haughtily above their fellows. The Cornish kept a suspicious eye on those who became preachers because, as the Cornish saying went, "the steps to the pulpit are the surest steps out of the mine." They objected to anyone who in rising forgot his origins, who forgot that he was the child of a miner and his hard-working wife. As a Methodist minister once wrote from Cornwall, "Uppish men are an abomination here." No one seemed to find Tregoning uppish, and despite the scrutiny of his community he played his leading role without giving offense.

Another long-time local preacher was William Lanyon, born in Cornwall in 1847. He began preaching at New Almaden as early as 1886, and like Tregoning he later affiliated with the Methodist Church in College Park.

In various years at New Almaden he took the part of Sunday School Superintendent, church steward and class leader. He and his wife Sarah had their faiths sorely tested in 1902 when their son, William Lanyon, Jr., was murdered in a saloon at the New Idria quicksilver mine in San Benito County. He was shot in the back while walking away from a quarrel. When news of the murder reached San Jose, fifty miles away, Lanyon rushed off to New Idria with the local sheriff, which left Sarah Lanyon to explain to a reporter what the son of a Methodist preacher was doing in a bar room on the Sabbath. Having learned the trade at New Almaden, he was a steady, industrious practical miner, she said, but he was also "fond of a good time." She told the reporter that she had a premonition of the young man's death, having seen him in a dream, lying in a pool of blood.

The most intriguing name on the roll of local preachers is Jane Vincent, who was appointed (probably by the Rev. Gafney) in 1872 at the age of about forty-four. Women preachers were rare in the California Conference, but not unknown. They would not have been unfamiliar to the immigrant congregation as John Wesley had occasionally used women preachers and one branch of British Methodism, the Primitive Methodists (who played a minor role in Cornwall) had prided itself on having "no sex limitation in church work." In the California Conference women lay preachers were not officially acknowledged until 1918, which probably means that in her day Jane Vincent had an extraordinary calling to preach. We regrettably know nothing more of this remarkable woman.

Another type of preaching at New Almaden was supplied by James Carlyon, born in Cornwall in 1842, one more common miner with a gift. He was the "exhorter" who would speak following the pastor's sermon, enlarging on the established theme and urging right conduct. He also led prayer meetings. During the time of the New Almaden church the ministry of the exhorter fell into disuse throughout the church in California.

9

Class Leaders, Faithful Guides

The Lord God has given me the tongue of a teacher,
that I may know how to sustain the weary with a word.
Isaiah, chapter 50

While most of the men, women and children in the Cornish camp heard the preachers regularly or at one time or another, only those who had full membership, or the nearly converted during their six months of probation, received tickets to attend the weekly class meetings. The pastor renewed the tickets quarterly on the recommendation of the class leaders. In class the faithful participated in prayer, Bible study, individual witness and discipline. The class leader, who knew the members intimately, interrogated each one regarding the state of his or her soul, and gave each one the necessary instruction, encouragement or reproof. One of Charles Wesley's hymns we sang at Methodist Church Day expresses the feeling of personal fellowship that informed the classes:

Jesus, united by Thy grace,
And each to each endeared,
With confidence we seek Thy face,
And know our prayer is heard.

Touched by the loadstone of Thy love,
Let all our hearts agree;
And ever towards each other move,
And ever move towards Thee.

Usually two classes met on Sunday mornings at New Almaden, one at eight and one at nine, each with twelve to thirty members. For many who attended, the meeting was an emblem of heaven and they prized their tickets.

Class meetings were an important part of evangelism. "All new converts should at once be inducted into this school of Christ," the Methodist newspaper recorded. "It will save them from backsliding." Responsible for this important work, the class leaders were virtually sub-pastors, appointed by the pastors and acting under them. In addition to leading the class, they visited the sick, met with the pastors and the stewards at a quarterly meeting, and collected and paid over the funds from the classes (traditionally a penny a week from each member). The leaders reported to the pastor when, usually due to illness or grief, members needed pastoral services in their homes. From the remaining church records we know that the leaders were all practical miners. (See appendix for a list of leaders and classes.) A man who was interrogated by his class leader on Sunday might work beside him in the stope on Monday.

A different kind of class met under the leadership of Mine Captain James Harry on Thursday evenings. If practice at New Almaden followed that in Cornwall, this class focused less on the Bible and introspection and more on reading and writing, probably with a view towards reading the Scriptures, though also with the possibility of people writing letters home or improving themselves in their work. The class members met for perhaps two hours of instruction after a ten-hour work day. In 1873 six women composed the class — Ann Smith, Mary Ann Pearce, Elizabeth Dunstan, Elizabeth Jeffrey, Eliza Pearce and Maria Bluett (who would have been about sixty). Within a few years it grew to twenty or more and included several men. (See appendix for a listing of class members). Though we have few records, we know that Harry led this class for as long as twenty-five years.

Education (as Methodist universities in the nations of the developed and developing worlds attest today) was a more or less natural consequence of the Methodist movement. The adult students in Captain Harry's class probably had some education as children, but the resources were limited. Growing up in Cornwall, they may have been taught in an Infant School (or "Dame School") where a partially-literate instructor drilled them on ABC's for a few pence a week. In England the instruction that common people received in Methodist classes made a significant contribution to the development of the working class and trade unions and to the greater participation in the community by people who could not attend a university. In America, where there was more opportunity, it helped immigrants to assimilate into the larger community, to move out of their initial occupations (such as mining) into a broader range of fields and professions. It encouraged them to put a high value on the education of their children, as New Almaden families did.

Preaching and teaching were not the only opportunities for leadership. Other lay officers of the church included the stewards and trustees.

Stewards were responsible for the money and various funds. Their ranks included miners, practical engineers, pumpmen and timbermen — all of them trusted. In addition to these there was at least one woman steward, Emma J. Miners; and at least one who was not of Cornish stock, Philip Bohemia, who lived at The Hacienda.

In addition to stewards, the church had trustees who met as a board to bear the responsibility for the church property and continuing operations. Their names, so far as we know them, are listed in Appendix 2. One of the notable trustees was John Goldsworthy, who contributed $500 to the building fund after the church burnt down in 1884 — an amount equal to more than six months of a miner's wages. Another prominent trustee was Captain James Varcoe, a supervisor in the mine under Captain Harry. He had wide experience, having mined in Cornwall, New Jersey, Michigan and Nevada, as well as at Grass Valley and New Idria, and he was trusted by both those he worked for and those who worked for him. In addition to his role in the church he was also a trustee of the Miners' Benevolent Society of New Almaden, the earliest mutual aid society formed on Mine Hill, organized and administered by the miners themselves. Its members paid $1 per month and their families received $10 a week when the member was sick and $100 on the member's death. (The Quicksilver Mining Company administered a Miners' Fund that also paid benefits and provided a doctor. All employees contributed to that fund through a payroll deduction.)

Before leaving the theme of education we should consider the influence of what Cornwall's great man of letters, Sir Arthur Quiller-Couch, referred to as "the scriptural habit." The mining families at New Almaden, even those who were but partially literate, were steeped in the Bible. They heard it read out weekly in church and many individuals read it daily. Families read the Bible aloud, often the father or mother reading, and children taking their turns as reader as soon as they could manage it. More than once in the depths of a tunnel a miner must have said, "Darkness is not dark to you, O God; the night is as bright as the day." More than once a miner's wife must have stepped out on a wooden porch to shake out a blanket, looked up to the peaks of the coastal mountains and thought, "I lift my eyes to the hills; from where is my help to come?"

The people of Mine Hill knew the heroic stories of the Old Testament, and the less heroic ones as well. To them Joseph's Egypt would have been nearer than Napoleon's France, and they knew more about King David than Charles I or Henry VIII. Their thoughts, their imaginings, even their speech (no matter how thick their dialect) would have been informed by

Biblical images and a Bible idiom. To at least partially share the consciousnesses of those miners one can learn the technical language of the mines, the meaning of Cornish words like "winzes" and "adits," and the English words that the Cornish converted to technical terms, like "sinkings," "levels," "risings," "crosscuts" and the "eyes of the mine"; or one can study the geology of California's coastal mountains, the unmetamorphosed Franciscian rock, the graywacke, siltstone, shale, and the intrusions of serpentine that hosted the quicksilver ore; or one can sing Methodist hymns and read the Bible.

Henry Tregoning - *Lay preacher and miner. Tregonong is pictured flasking mercury. (Archives, The History Museums of San Jose).*

10

A Church for Children

The wolf shall live with the lamb,
the leopard shall lie down with the kid,
the calf and the lion and the fatling together,
and a little child shall lead them.
Isaiah, Chapter 11

From the earliest days of the New Almaden church the religious activities of children centered on their Sunday classes. The Methodists did not invent Sunday School, but they quickly saw its value and adopted it, and from an early date John Wesley required his traveling preachers to gather the children into catechism classes. In 1776 at Redruth, Cornwall, Wesley addressed a group of fifty or sixty children and wrote afterwards, "How much depends upon these! All the hope of the rising generation."

On Sunday at New Almaden about 165 children attended religious classes in the church basement for about two hours in the morning and perhaps another hour or two in the afternoon. In 1887 the Rev. Trefren gave his appraisal:

> I want to say this, that I have never preached to a better, more intelligent appearing congregation, better behaved congregation, better dressed, and apparently better fed; our Sunday school is an extra Sunday school, if you please: they are well officered; they have good teachers; it is very regularly and well attended, and they are better versed in the Scriptures than is usual in Sunday schools even.

We have a good account of what the boys wore on Sunday from William Trevorrow:

> Sunday forenoon, boys would wear clean every-day clothes, but after the noon dinner they would change to their "Sunday best" store clothes, and then on to Sunday school where there were boys and also girls classes, and Bible classes for the grown-ups who attended. I learned much of Bible history from Mr. William Reed and Mr. Edwin Tregoning. Then a walk along the new road and home to "tea" (supper), before we went to church. Never were clothes so carefully guarded. Monday mornings, before

washing by hand the week's clothes, mother would brush the suit and carefully fold it away in a bureau drawer not to be worn again until the next Sunday.

In addition to the one on the hill, there was a second Sunday school held in the school house at The Hacienda or on sunny days on the wide lawn at La Casa Grande. For many years Mrs. James Randol, wife of the general manager, was its benefactress. When she left New Almaden in 1886, the children presented her with a scroll that read in part:

Your presence and general disposition have brought blessing, and sunshine, to our hearts, and lives; and your kindly attention, and unsparing generosity towards us has laid us under obligations that we cannot discharge.

Though it took a hand other than a child's to write something so obsequious, we can imagine that the children appended their signatures with genuine gratitude. The thirty-eight little signatories included several groups of siblings, many Cornish children, and offspring of the mine management, such as Alma, George, Lottie, David and Arthur Bulmore. (Robert Bulmore, their father, was cashier of the mining company). One child signed "John Hancock," but it wasn't a prank as John was the brother of Ellen and Joseph, and son of Joseph and Emma Hancock. His Cornish father had died in a mining accident a few years before.

The women on the hill probably played an important role in teaching the children, relying on materials published by the Methodist church. An article in the California *Christian Advocate* described the teacher's duties. "Interest your class in the lesson of the hour," it read, "because you have first become interested in it yourself, because you have been planning, before-hand, is how you shall interest them." The duties continued,

To gather and keep a class about you, not merely to teach those who happen to be present. You can easily enough gather a class, by a word of introduction to the boys and girls playing in your streets, who do not go to Sunday school. You can only keep a class by making them feel, both in the school and out of the school, that you are interested in them. Greet them with kind words whenever you meet them. Hunt them up as soon as they become regular in attendance.

Since we have found no Sunday School records, our knowledge of the classes or methods is limited. We do know that when Bishop E. O. Haven visited New Almaden in 1881 he found that the children were uniformly healthy and as intelligent as any he had seen. "The Sabbath school is a model," he wrote in a brief account. "The church seems to be a great family, made up of all the families of that faith in the village." What we know of the school beside this is largely anecdotal. Since Santa Clara County provided an education for the children in the school house on Mine Hill, the Sunday School did not have the burden of trying to teach them to read and write, as it originally did in England and Cornwall. In classes children were perhaps told that they were being trained for heaven. They sometimes memorized Bible verses and hymns and perhaps this ditty that was popular in Cornish churches:

> Then children, attend to the words you repeat,
> And always remember this line:
> 'Tis a credit to any good girl to be neat,
> But quite a disgrace to be fine.

Several of the pastors took a special interest in the children on Mine Hill. In April 1892 the Rev. Bryant organized a probationers class of forty children and in the next year at least fifteen of them were received as full members. Some children showed a special affinity for the spiritual life, such as eleven-year-old Selina Odgers who impressed the Rev. Joseph R. Wolfe. "This girl came to the parsonage February 18, 1893," he wrote, "and wanted me to put her on the probation list." Selina was received as a full member of the church the following October. One minister took time to sign the autograph book belonging to Jemima May Andrew:

> Dear Friend, Choose the better part,
> ere it be too late, is the wish of your friend.
> *[The Rev.] W. J. Peters.*
> New Almaden, March 20, 1896

For the Sunday school children the holidays were a delight and one of the best remembered was Christmas of 1875. An entertainment on the hill a week before raised enough money to provide for a Christmas tree in the church and the young and old of the camp brought presents to hang on its boughs. "At 7:00 [on Christmas Eve] the little church was full and never a more beautiful sight was seen upon our Hill than our ladened down evergreen with its hundreds of pretty and useful presents." After the service several of the Sunday school children recited and then the gifts were distributed. Santa Claus arrived "and was very liberal with his candy, giving to each little one at least a pound!" That same Christmas the members of the Methodist Church presented a Bible to Mr. and Mrs. Randol.

Lotty Tonkin and her sister Elizabeth Tonkin Colliver remembered the Christmases they spent on Mine Hill in the 1890s. About a week before Christmas a choir of Cornish miners, finding the path by lantern light, would go from door to door singing carols. Probably they sang lesser-known carols that were popular in Cornwall, such as "Lo the eastern sages rise," and "Hark what music fills creation," as well as Charles Wesley's "Hark! the Herald-Angels Sing," and many others. After singing they would be invited in, usually for the customary saffron cake and tea, and according to the Tonkin daughters, often "something stronger than tea." In their wood stoves the women had already begun baking homemade fruit cakes, candy, more saffron cakes and figgy-duff cookies. "It was very pioneerish," they recalled.

> We'd kill the turkey for Christmas Day dinner. There was plum pudding and a dressing of bread crumbs, suet and thyme from the garden. It gave real flavor to the bird. We'd pick the thyme and clean off all the little fine leaves.

On Christmas day, Laurence Bulmore and Milton Lanyon remembered in their book *Cinnabar Hills*, the residents assembled at the store where adults performed a variety of Christmas music and the school children offered a program under the direction of their teachers. The evening might include more caroling. The night after Christmas, in keeping with a Cornish custom, the children would wear masks or blacken their faces and do pranks, and they would expect refreshments or small gifts.

Other holidays punctuated the children's year. Washington's Birthday was commemorated with a church tea in the afternoon, usually followed by an entertainment at night. Good Friday was sometimes marked by a tea. Easter Sunday was a feast day in the church and in the homes and boarding houses on the hill. "Mother would roast a hind quarter of a very young lamb," William Trevorrow remembered, "and that day would serve our first green peas and potatoes of the season." On Thanksgiving Day a tea was held at the church.

On May 30 the children enjoyed the annual tea treat, a Cornish custom. (This may have been combined with what the California Conference called "Children's Day," a day when the Conference asked the local churches to emphasize reading and writing.) In the old country the treats were limited to a cup of tea and a saffron bun, but New Almaden afforded more elaborate fare. On Mine Hill the day began with a parade and a brass band that led the children through the dusty streets of the Cornish camp and arrived at the base of a great oak tree at the rear of the church. There the children feasted at a pot-luck picnic, as William Trevorrow well remembered:

> The one day of the year that provisions, cooked, were sent from San Jose. I never since have tasted such excellent baked ham, and the cakes and baker's "milk" bread, etc., were long thought of with much appreciation. After the "Treat" games were played by the young. Kissing ring was most popular. Cornish folk, young or old, are very fond of a bit of kissin'. In the evening some noted preacher from "away" preached, and his words were absorbed with reverence.

Trevorrow left out the clotted cream his mother made for these occasions from an old country recipe.

New Almaden children, 1888 - The children, who attended the public school on Mine Hill during the week, attended Sunday school at the Methodist church. At the time this photograph was taken about 300 children lived in English Camp. Santa Clara County operated the school.
(New Almaden Museum)

11

English Town Commonwealth

Happy is the nation whose God is the Lord!
Happy the people he has chosen to be his own!
Psalm 33

To begin to understand the common life of the English-speaking settlement on Mine Hill we must return to an analytical mode and consider some of the concepts and ideas that informed Methodism from its beginning. As preachers and ministers John and Charles Wesley rejected root and branch the Calvinist idea of predestination, a central doctrine of English Puritanism. The restriction of God's grace to an elect few was repugnant to the Methodists because it contradicted their sense of the New Testament and made nonsense of the spiritual life. Methodism, nevertheless, and especially as it was practiced in Cornwall, incorporated a kind of discipline that can only be described as Puritan. A scholar's description of early Methodists makes the point:

> They were frugal, industrious, conscientious, sabbatarian; strict, and sometimes narrow and prudish, in their morals; stern in the bringing up of their children; averse from entertainments and unrestrained laughter. So far they were staunch representatives of the Puritan tradition which has never died out in England, unless it has done so recently. But those who had really caught the meaning of Wesley's message had something else about them also: an inward, serene gaiety which comes out over and over again in Charles Wesley's hymns, springing from the joyful assurance of salvation which Calvinism fails to give. And, as a result, the Methodists knew not only how to face hardship and scorn without being much troubled, but also how to die. [Rupert E. Davis, *Methodism* (1963, 1985), page 80].

When one Mine Hill descendant recalls that her family was "straight-laced and Wesleyan," she alludes to that in-dwelling Puritanism that had came across the ocean like the sprigs of periwinkle that the Cornish planted around their cabins and that still flourish on Mine Hill today. At New Almaden Cornish Methodism imposed an ascetic discipline that called for regular attendance at preaching, the sacraments, and class meetings.

In such a small, homogeneous community there must have been considerable pressure to conform. Believers renounced such pleasures as sports, revels, theater, idle (that is, non-religious) songs, cards and dancing. Young men wore short hair and young women cut their curls, and even as the strictures lessened no young woman would become so worldly as to wear ribbons in her bonnet.

Even speech patterns changed as a result of the discipline. Having spent many hours looking up to American-born pastors in their pulpits, the church members came to frown on the Cornish dialect, preferring a more educated American English. These people, who had been schooled in their pews, let the proper English expression — "He is one of our family" — replace their Cornish expression — " 'e do belong t' we" — and thereby mastered the speech of mainstream America. In the bargain they lost a version of English that retained some of the rhythm and intonations of the old Cornish language, a language their forebears had spoken for centuries. They lost something of Cornwall to gain California.

Though the community on Mine Hill had an insular quality, as did Cornwall itself, the residents had daily and weekly reports from the wider world. More than thirty families subscribed to The California *Christian Advocate*, the Methodist newspaper published in San Francisco, and from them it probably passed around the camp. The *Advocate* dealt with religious news along with wider social issues and it provided summaries of articles (crimes stories, for example) from secular newspapers. As did all California newspapers it carried mining news, reports of discoveries and values of precious metals. It analyzed the annual reports of the Quicksilver Mining Company, giving the miners at New Almaden an objective source of information about their employer. It also contained stories for children, poems, obituaries of the faithful, and advertisements. One of the interesting ads promoted Wistar's Balsam of Wild Cherry Cough Syrup, which claimed to cure consumption. Many in the Cornish camp subscribed to other Methodist newspapers and publications as well as to secular newspapers. By the mid-1880s about forty copies of the San Francisco *Chronicle* arrived every day and some subscribed by mail to the newspapers from home, including Cornwall's *West Briton*.

Temperance was the familiar face of Methodism during the years of the Mine Hill church , and in the six decades since the repeal of Prohibition the popular image of the teetoling Methodist has not entirely faded away. In the nineteenth century Methodist ministers throughout their travels saw the effects of drunkenness and they deplored it. Methodist

English Camp and Church - *For its predominantly Cornish families, the English-speaking camp provided a stable enviroment. The miners accepted lower wages than they might have earned in gold or silver mining camps in the Sierra-Nevada to work in mercury mining at New Almaden, where their children could enjoy a family-oriented community with a church and school.(Archives, The History Museums of San Jose).*

laymen, and especially laywomen, saw the debilitating influence of drink on their fellows and mates, and they saw liquor as the common denominator of the country's social ills. Temperance became a crusade, abstinence was an ideal, grape juice replaced wine in the church. Many at New Almaden and elsewhere were supported in their attitudes by regular articles in the California *Christian Advocate* that evolved into a Temperance page. Men on Mine Hill organized a lodge of Good Templers, a fraternal temperance society and with their wives they may have attended temperance lectures, such as the ones sponsored regularly in San Jose by the Methodists and other Protestant denominations.

As not all of the quicksilver miners heeded the warnings against drink, the church and the saloon became the poles of community life. When some of the miners took the stage into San Jose they frequented the saloon owned by Charlie Barr on First at El Dorado streets (now called Post). William Trevorrow, no more than a boy, had his first taste of steam beer standing at the bar beside his Grandfather Geach in Old Joe's Brewery in San Jose. The night after the church burned three Cornishmen were arrested at Jacob Haub's saloon on Market Street for disturbing the peace. Nearer the mine a saloon operated on Almaden Road, north of the mining company's property, at one time under the management of an Irish immigrant, and at another under Edward Arents, a Welshman. The company exerted its influence to have the saloon closed on Sunday evenings to assure that workers would report to work on Mondays. The company store also sold beer, wine and liquor, but there were no saloons at Cornish camp. There were saloons and gambling near enough at the Mexican camp.

Abstinence pledges were popular at New Almaden, but not everyone was willing. Such a pledge was printed in the front-matter of miner John Drew's family Bible, but no one bothered to sign. One who did make a pledge, after another sort of baptism, was young Dick Pearce. In 1871 when he was ten he sampled the keg at a welcoming party for Captain James Harry, and then with some of his fellows he performed a dance on a water tank that drew the wrong kind of attention. Attempting to escape his irate father, Dick slipped down a narrow ravine and tumbled into a blackberry thicket. His father eventually caught up with him. Before the night was over, scratched, bruised and remorseful, Dick swore off hard liquor. He stuck to his pledge for the rest of his life.

Temperance could cause dissension not just in the community but within families, as evinced by the lives of Henry and Eliza James. Both of Cornish stock, they came from the old country when young. They met at New Almaden and married in the church: he age thirty-eight;

she, twenty-seven. They were strict Methodists, never played cards, never danced. On the Sabbath they read only the Bible, *The Advocate* or other religious literature. They didn't drink, though over his wife's objections he kept a partially consumed bottle of brandy on a high shelf, a totem of masculine independence. Eliza James' consternation over that bottle lasted until the day her husband was buried. Immediately on returning home from the funeral she pushed a chair under the shelf, took the bottle and poured it down the sink.

An especially unattractive aspect of the camp to our more ecumenical age was the prevailing attitude towards Roman Catholics. (Such attitudes did not come from Wesley). The Cornish had an aversion to the church of Rome and concluded that the relative poverty of their Hispanic neighbors was partly a consequence of its teachings. One explanation as to why the Cornish were predominantly Republicans was that they associated the Democrats with the Irish and the Irish with Catholicism. The antipathy, though, was not unmitigated. Thomas Hicks, who promoted the building of Hicks Road, married Josefa Bernal in his wife's church and saw his ten children baptized by the priest. He was just one of several Cornishmen who married Mexican or Californio women. The residents of English camp and the nearby Spanish camp, home to at least 1,200 Hispanic miners, women and children, jointly celebrated holidays, except for Christmas, owing to their different traditions. For sheer color the Cornish children valued the Catholic observances over their own, and the adventuresome Dick Pearce never forgot witnessing the "Buena Noche" procession on Christmas Eve, when men carried statuettes depicting Mary and Joseph looking for a place to stay. He vividly recalled the burning of Judas in effigy on Holy Saturday. Sometimes, winning the Cornish children's further admiration, Judas' wife and children were also burned.

Wesley knew something of the Cornish. "Many of them have little sense and a great inclination to criticize," he said. For all their traveling across oceans and continents, the Cornish often traveled from one mining camp to another and this was not necessarily broadening. Their narrowness, to be fair, was at times a justified reaction to the life around them, to poverty, slim opportunities, harsh working conditions, the immediacy of death. There was little margin for error as what we would call a social safety net in our community was barely a strand of yarn in theirs. We should not measure their community, though, just at its narrowest points of strictures or taboo when there were also broader points of charity and toleration. Perhaps no one better reflected the charity of this community than did Louisa Rowe Varcoe, New Almaden's "angel of mercy."

"Auntie" Varcoe, as all the children called her, was born in Cornwall about 1842 and came to New Almaden in her late twenties and there married Captain James Varcoe. Judge A. C. Innes, a long-time New Almaden figure, described her:

> Day or night, rain or shine, Almaden's messenger of mercy was there, to comfort the afflicted, to console the widow, and ease the heart-sobs of fatherless children. Mrs. Varcoe possessed in high degree that rare faculty of being able to do things while most people were simply appalled, her hand worked in unison with her heart. . . . her memory will be cherished as a beautiful example of the everyday-all-the-time, noble Christian woman.

The Company Store - From the 1850s to the 1880s men and women and even children on Mine Hill recognized the store as a symbol of oppression and the church as a symbol of hope. (See pages 69-70). The brick building was constructed in 1864. (New Almaden Museum).

12

Wesleyan Workers

Forth in thy name, O Lord, I go,
My daily labor to pursue,
Thee, only thee resolved to know
In all I think, or speak, or do.
Charles Wesley, hymn

As a consequence of emphasizing the reformation of the individual, personal austerity and scriptural obedience, Methodism created desirable workers. From the early days of the revival John Wesley taught his followers to be industrious, claiming (with obvious hyperbole) that his societies drove out an idle person as they would a thief or a murderer. By teaching individuals to accept their work as a divine calling, Methodism gave them strength of purpose. It upheld the morality of the economic order and this no doubt pleased Randol and the officers and managers of the mining company. Whatever else the church on the hill represented to the management, at a minimum the white-washed boards and high steeple were emblematic of a stable, law-abiding, industrious work-force. The management was perhaps as proud of the church as they were of another prominent structure, the great iron shed with its three smoking chimneys that housed the Cornish pump at the Buena Vista shaft.

No matter how deeply the economics of their stations divided them, the general manager and his workers at New Almaden were bound together by common ethical and religious values. "English Town," as the company styled the dusty camp, was often remembered as idyllic, a colony of contented working families under the paternal eye of a resident manager and a few hired professionals. "The climate being balmy, the school for children excellent, and the Methodist Church associations being good for families," William Trevorrow remembered, "New Almaden Hill was a family mining camp and married men did not often seek employment elsewhere." Yet as in other idylls, all was not as it appeared. Corruption could be unearthed as was the cinnabar ore. Conflict surfaced when the miners struck in 1865 and continued long afterwards. Much of the conflict centered around the company store.

Russell Pearce, whose ancestors were ministers and miners, learned from his grandfather how the company store at New Almaden created dissension that eventually involved the church. Pearce explained it at Methodist Church Day in May 1995, the event where this account of the church began. In Nevada in the 1880s miners earned a minimum of four dollars a day, while at the same time at New Almaden miners on contract averaged as little as $2.48. In addition, Mine Hill residents were expected to patronize the company store where prices were twenty-five per cent higher than in San Jose. The situation left little money for families or for the church. When they could every family or single member of the church contributed a dollar a month, and non-members usually fifty cents, to pay the pastor's salary and maintain the operation. Under such conditions even this modest level of support was not always possible. The daughters of the Rev. F. M. Willis, who served at New Almaden from 1885 - 86, called it "the poorest place they ever were in."

Willis, who had known countless mining camps and had even done some mining himself, fully appreciated the plight of the workers and decided to make a stand for them and for his family. In 1886 he resigned his charge as a protest against the company's practices. The act, Pearce said , had a strong impact: "The church appeared as a whitened sepulcher." In the following year the company's practices received more notoriety as the result of an investigation pertaining to a Congressional election. Conditions and wages improved after that and after twenty-odd years of exploitation the company store became competitive with stores in San Jose.

Even when economic conditions improved, the men of the Cornish camp were still working in one of the world's most dangerous occupations. (In our own time, with all of our safety standards and regulations, mining remains extremely dangerous.) There is no complete accounting of the casualties on Mine Hill, but there were many and many close calls. Tregoning and John Drew, to give one example, nearly suffocated when the cage in which they were riding got stuck in the shaft in an area flooded with carbon dioxide. A frantic engineer above was able to free the cage in time. Several others were not so lucky, such as Charles Harris who, his pastor recorded in August 1891, died in a cave-in. Given the obvious dangers, the role that faith played in giving men the courage to go underground day after day and year after year can hardly be underestimated.

13

"Claims to be Episcopal"

*"I truly understand that God shows no partiality,
but in every nation anyone who fears him
and does what is right is acceptable to him."*
Acts, Chapter 10

Louisa Pearce, mother of Dick Pearce, was listed as a "Member in Full Connection" in the log of the New Almaden Methodist Church, and beside her name appears the notation, "Claims to be Episcopal." It was not an uncommon assertion and in Mrs. Pearce's case it was substantiated by the fact that she was confirmed and married in St. Uny's parish church (that is, Anglican church) in Redruth, Cornwall, at the foot of Carn Brea hill. Methodism began as a movement within the Anglican church in England and Wesley insisted on regular church attendance. In many Cornish churches the Methodists were recognized as the ones rushing away after the service, hurrying to attend the preaching in their nearby meeting house. Even into the twentieth century in Cornwall (and in some other localities) many went to Anglican church services on Sunday morning and heard preaching in the Methodist chapel in the afternoon. Today in the old country one still hears the question, "Are you church or chapel?"

Several of the Mine Hill families, including the Cornish, Doble, Drew, Faull, James, Harvey, Pearce, Trengove and Willoughby families maintained connections with Trinity Episcopal Church (now Cathedral) in San Jose, the Episcopal Church being the American branch of the Anglican. Thomas Drew had been married at the parish church in Truro, Cornwall (St. Mary's Church before it was transformed into the present cathedral) — his descendants found his name in the registry there. In 1891 his son John married Sarah Bishop at Trinity in San Jose. Richard Faull was a member of the Methodist Church on Mine Hill when he married Susan Tressider at Trinity in 1877 and his daughter Mildred Maria was baptized and confirmed at Trinity. His brothers Captain Thomas and James, his sister-in-law Jane and his niece Minnie Faull were all buried at Oak Hill Cemetery in San Jose following Episcopal services. Several couples were married at Trinity and then had their children baptized at the Methodist

Church, including William and Emily Gray Cornish, Samual and Bessie James, Thomas and Elizabeth Trengove Harvey, and Elijah and Mary Trengove. Edwin Willoughby was a local preacher and Ann Billings was a member of the Methodist Church when they elected to marry at Trinity in 1880.

While there is not sufficient information to identify a pattern, it seems likely that some of these families relied less on Trinity Church, a dusty stage ride away in San Jose, after a Methodist minister was assigned to the Cornish camp, and especially after the church was erected in 1875. At the least it was more convenient to have infants baptized on Mine Hill rather than taking them to town, and given the prospect of infant mortality, more sure. New Almaden people continued to be buried from Trinity Church into the twentieth century, including Jane Doble in 1901 and James Kelly (a Cornish Kelly) in 1902. Some families, like the Faulls and Paulls, affiliated with Trinity after leaving the mining camp and moving into town. (Jan Paull, a New Almaden descendant, is the parish historian there today.)

While the first religious services in the Cornish camp were Methodist, the services at the Hacienda may have been read from the Episcopal Book of Common Prayer. This would have been the preference of the Randols, who were apparently Episcopalians (judging from the fact that James Randol's brother, Dr. A. R. Randol, was buried from Trinity Church in 1876), and of Bulmore, who was English. The mining company officers and their families apparently read Morning Prayer on Sunday until about 1880 when a Methodist service and Sunday school were organized at the foot of Mine Hill, and then prayer and preaching presumably replaced the morning office.

14

Born In Song

The mountains and the hills before you
shall burst into song, and all the trees
of the field shall clap their hands.
Isaiah 55

When Methodists gather they are likely to sing hymns by Charles Wesley. People sang them on Methodist Church Day, the rainy day in May where this story began, carrying on a Cornish, as well as a Methodist, tradition. Like other Celtic people the Cornish are exceedingly fond of music, their taste in past generations running towards the choirs and brass bands that one can still hear throughout the old country. For two hundred years — at least from the time of the Wesleys to the age of radio — hymns were the popular music of the working people, and in the music and lyrics the Cornish found expression for their deepest convictions.

Anyone visiting Cornish camp in its day would have recognized that music was central to the life there. A reporter from San Francisco described the choir he found there in 1883:

> I visited the church on a Saturday afternoon. It is a clean, well-cared-for building, and already the organist and choir were rehearsing the hymns for the succeeding day. The subdued strains of that hymnic invocation, one of the earliest as well as the best in the Methodist collection,
>
> > "Leader of faithful souls and guide
> > Of all that travel to the sky,"
>
> floated out on the still air. There are many very good voices among the miners — the parent sings a manly bass or baritone, the daughters contribute a rich soprano or mezzo, that harmonizes with the boyish contralto of younger members of the family. Pretty nearly all the miners go to church on Sunday; that is, when they are above ground.

We should not think of these singers as tuneless primitives. As the wife of an Eastern mining engineer noted, the Cornish sang as if they were all the children of choir masters.

There was no choir master at New Almaden but instead a young woman of remarkable talents — Emma Morcum Tregoning. A central figure in the church, she was the organist and choir director as well as the camp's contralto singer. She also led the Sunday School entertainments. She was born in Par, Cornwall in 1861 and at nineteen married in the New Almaden church to Edwin Tregoning. Hers was a musical family. The Tregoning house was a regular source of music on Sunday evenings when many of the camp's musicians would gather on the porch and men and families would crowd around to join in singing. Along with hymns and carols, they also sang folk songs from home:

> Pasty, role out like a plate
> Baked with turmets, tates and mate
> Crumpled up and baked like fate —
> That's a Cornish pasty.

Emma Tregoning lived out her life in northern California. In her eighties she was spry enough to climb into a tree to pick apricots for her grand-daughter.

The hill was a musical place. The miners would sing as the cage descended in the shaft and the tributers, who were paid for their ore rather than their time, might sing for an hour before beginning their work. According to tradition a miner in peril sings heavenward and by following his song his coworkers might rescue him. One of the memorable singers was Jimmy Johns, a deep-voiced Cornish miner, a bachelor, a stalwart Methodist who resided at Pearce's boarding house. Many heard his voice in the depth of the mine as well as in the church. The women were equally musical and a family that had daughters often tried to acquire a small organ. Emma Tregoning might give the lessons. Another prominent musician, Emily Collins Pearce, taught piano on the hill for more than twenty years. She passed on her music to her own children, including her son, Russell, who rode the stage into San Jose three times a week to take violin lessons from Wesley Toy. When the Pearce family moved into San Jose, as most of the Mine Hill families did around the turn of the Twentieth Century, Emily Pearce became the organist at the First Methodist Church.

Musical patterns in Methodist worship were developing during the era of the New Almaden church and changes in music reflected wider changes in the worship. In the early days of the movement John Wesley cautioned his followers to beware of formality in music and the Methodists promoted hymns that everyone could sing, encouraging each believer to make a joyful noise to the Lord. By the New Almaden era, though, church choirs were emerging as a predominant force in Methodist worship and music was gradually becoming the property of trained musicians. A new hymnal in 1878 included occasional pieces and chants, including traditional Psalter texts with their Latin titles, "Venite," "Te Deum," "Magnificat," and others. The entire congregation still sang the familiar hymns, including those by Charles Wesley, Isaac Watts, William Cowper, and many more. At other times, though, the congregation was the audience as the choir performed oratorios from Handel and possibly older Anglican church music from Purcell, Byrd and Tallis.

As the music changed, so did the worship, tending towards formality. The Liturgical year, largely ignored by the Frontier church, was re-established in the Methodist Church of this time through the hymnals, especially through hymns for special days. With the publication of the 1905 hymnal the Methodists had in their hands all the elements for a liturgical form of public worship, though the extent to which they used it depended on the individual pastor. For sure the days of Camp Meetings and "howling Methodists" were gone, and the passing was regretted by many who had their faith rekindled in such settings. Methodism was crowning its working class roots with a flowering of Victorian respectability. As its members moved into towns and rose into the trades and the professions, it was gradually leaving the frontier and the mining camp behind.

Emma Morcum Tregoning - *Organist and music director.*
(Tregoning-Trevorrow family).

75

15

Last Years, 1898 - 1914

Send out your light and your truth, that they may lead me,
and bring me to your holy hill and to your dwelling.
Psalm 43

The end of profitable mining was in sight at the time that general manager James Randol left Almaden in 1890. In the preceding years much of the mine's wealth had come up the mine's prominent Randol Shaft, but by the late 1880s the future of the mine depended on finding new sources of cinnabar ore and the miners hollowed miles and miles of tunnels and shafts in the search. During the 1890s new shafts, like the Harry and the Santa Maria, provided enough good ore to keep the mine solvent and in some years profitable. Yet even with the future of the mine uncertain, the life of the Methodist church at New Almaden flourished, and especially under the leadership of the Rev. J. W. Bryant, who brought more members into the church than any other minister. During his time on the hill (1890-92) 101 people, including forty children, attended probationer classes and fifty-three of them were received into full membership. At the end of the decade, though, mine production diminished, the workers and their families moved on, church membership plummeted. The Rev. J. W. Buxton, who served two tours of duty, longer than anyone else at New Almaden, saw membership fall from about eighty in 1898 to only fifty in 1902.

About the ministers who served New Almaden during the declining years we know little, and about Edwin Harry Smith, who served there in 1903, we know least. He was born in Hamilton, Missouri and was a probationary minister in the California Conference when he came to Mine Hill. There he earned $800 a year, baptized six children and had seventeen probationers in a class. He wrote of New Almaden,

> There has been practically no change here in the last ten years. The charge
> has been well served and is seemingly in good condition, but there have
> been no conversions to speak of. There is a list of young people here, but
> only a few in the church. We are determined by the help of God to change
> this, or move on.

Apparently he had some success because he got seventeen probationers in a class and saw the number of full members increase to 80, the best showing in several years. Smith turned the work over to the Rev. Theodore Taylor, whose outstanding singing voice was probably much appreciated. The Rev. M. J. Gough was probably the last of the ministers to reside at New Almaden (1907-1908). Born in England, once a student of medicine, he won only the faint praise of his colleagues: "He was one of a host of humble, undistinguished men who will find an abundant welcome in the Heavenly City."

Three young men, A. H. Clark (1908-09), C. J. Irwin (1909-10) and J. Wesley Richards (1910-11), closed out the ministry at New Almaden, though probably none of them actually resided on Mine Hill. Richards, for example, was affiliated with the College of the Pacific in San Jose and may have gone to New Almaden to preach two or more times a month. During his tenure a visitor to New Almaden named Maria Branard sent a picture postcard of the church to her daughter in San Francisco, writing on the back:

New Almaden, June 7, 1909. Dear Daughter, This is where I went to Sunday School and church yesterday. There were 18 at the Sunday school and 18 at church. . . .

In succeeding years the number of full members shrank to thirty-four, to eight and finally to one. No infants disturbed the baptismal water. In 1912 the Quicksilver Mining Company declared bankruptcy and from 1912-14 the Conference did not appoint a minister but left New Almaden "to be supplied." Eventually services ceased and in September 1914 the Methodist Annual Conference divided the remaining $10 in the New Almaden treasury between mission work and the pension fund for pastors and pastors' wives. The church was abandoned, retaining its place only as a ruin on the hill. In the 1930s the Civilian Conservation Corps moved into the area and tore the church down, salvaging the usable materials.

Even as worship services were declining at New Almaden, the mining families were taking letters from their pastor and transferring their membership to churches in San Jose. The Centella Church at South Second and Reed streets took in the Willoughby, Mitchell and Gray families and Edna May Drew. The families that moved to the First Methodist Church fill at least five pages of tightly written notes and included such names as Argall, Bennett, Collins, English, Johns, Polglase, Tonkin, Toy, and Wellington. Mattie Drew, Frank Argall and W. H. Tonkin were among the Sunday School teachers, Dean Drew was an usher, and Mrs. Harry James was president of the Woman's Foreign Missionary Society. A clutch of children who had been schooled on Mine Hill joined the young adult's organization, the Epworth League, when they got into town. From the San Jose records we see some of the New Almadeners transferring to Methodist churches throughout the Bay Area and California or even leaving the Methodists for the Presbyterians, Lutherans or Episcopalians.

Through the advertisements in the San Jose church directory we see the immigrant Methodists finding their way into the economic life of the city. H. J. Pascoe became the plumber, George English the carpenter, and Hocking and Williams the funeral directors, and probably their first customers were Methodists. Frank Pascoe had the coffee, tea and spice shop and Ed James sold glass. Argall and Bennett became dentists and three Drew sons went into banking. Education was a popular choice and several men and women, including my great grandmother, prepared for teaching careers at the state normal school (now San Jose State University). Any work that involved engineering had appeal and several found work in foundaries and blacksmith or machine shops. Some had saved to buy property and plant orchards. Whatever calling they followed, each Sunday they gathered at the church to maintain the friendships and connections they knew on Mine Hill and to make new ones.

By that time the Methodist Episcopal Church at New Almaden had become a memory, living on in its people, in the stories that passed down. It lived on, too, in the ministry of the Rev. George Colliver, who grew up on Mine Hill to become a respected pastor and an authority on Christian education, teaching at the University of the Pacific. The old church lives on as well in the minds of hikers who climb the trail through the Quicksilver County Park to see where it once stood and from that spot to enjoy the views of the Santa Clara Valley, the Santa Teresa Hills, the Hamilton Range and the bay. It lives on in the descendants of the old church who brought their stories to Methodist Church Day and in the hearts of local Methodists, who carry on the work of the church, the preaching and singing, prayers and breaking of bread. It lives on in the imaginations of the youngest descendants, the children, who came and heard the stories, sang the hymns and met two women in their nineties who once were little girls in the pews of the old church.

One hundred or more years ago when one of the faithful died at New Almaden, it was common for the pastor to write an obituary that would appear in the pages of the California *Christian Advocate*. In 1878 when miner John Tregoning died, age 58, the Rev. Hopkins wrote,

He died in great peace, with full confidence of a blessed immortality. He leaves a wife and four children, two daughters and two sons, both local preachers and earnest Christian workers. May this whole family, mother, and children, be an unbroken family in the kingdom of glory.

In that kingdom, where brokeness is mended, may the whole family of the New Almaden church gather on a hill. And may we who remain value the heritage that comes to us from people who, acknowledging God's grace, lived lives full of purpose. May we always prize the memory of people who followed their hope across the ocean, who found hope even in the darkness of the mine, and who died in the hope they shared with "Mr. Westley" and with all faithful people throughout the generations.

Women at the church, 1919 - Two unidentified women in Edwardian dress visit the derelict church at New Almaden five years after it closed. A brace in the foreground is propping up the eastern wall of the church. (John Slenter Collection).

Appendix 1

THE NEW ALMADEN METHODIST-EPISCOPAL CHURCH — PASTORS

Pastors Assigned to the Santa Clara Circuit
(eventually including Los Gatos and New Almaden)

Isaac Owen	1856 - 1857
I. Owen & Wm. Gafney	1857 - 1858
James W. Brier	1858 - 1859
J. Pettit & Colin Anderson	1859 - 1860
John Sharp	1860 - 1861
R. R. Dunlap	1861 - 1862
Edward Adams Hazen	1863 - 1865
Wm. Morrow, M. D.	1865 - 1867
W. B. Priddy	1867 - 1868
James Corwin	1868 - 1869
H. Gibson & F. D. Hodgram	1869 - 1870
H. Gibson	1870 - 1871

Pastors Assigned to Los Gatos
(responsible for Los Gatos, Guadalupe and New Almaden)

A. C. Hazzard	1871 - 1872
William Gafney	1872 - 1875
T. B. Hopkins	1875 - 1878
R. W. Williams	1878 - 1879
Jessie J. Smith	1879 - 1881

Pastors Assigned to New Almaden

George W. Beatty	1879 - 1881
J. H. Wythe, Jr.	1881 - 1882
C. G. Milne	1883 - 1883
J. S. Fisher	1883 - 1884
"to be supplied"	1884

F. M. Willis	1885 - 1886
J. Lewis Trefren	1886 - 1888
H. C. Benson, DD.	1888 - 1890
J. W. Bryant	1890 - 1892
J. R. Wolfe	1892 - 1894
W. J. Peters	1895 - 1898
J. W. Buxton	1898 - 1902
E. H. Smith	1903
Theodore Taylor	1904
W. S. Urmy, DD	1905
J. W. Buxton	1906
M. J. Gough	1907
A. H. Clark	1908
C. J. Irwin	1909
J. Wesley Richards	1910 - 1911
"to be supplied"	1912 - 1914

Pastors Associated with New Almaden

C. V. Anthony	Gave sermon of dedication, Easter 1875
George H. Colliver	Raised at New Almaden

George H. Colliver - *A child of Mine Hill and a Methodist pastor.*
(Archives, United Methodist Church, Berkeley & Stockton)

Appendix 2

THE NEW ALMADEN METHODIST-EPISCOPAL CHURCH — LAY LEADERS

Local Preachers

Rhodes Gardner
W. F. Gray
William Lanyon
Thomas H. Morcum
Charles Prisk
William Stiles
Henry Tregoning
John Trevorrow
Thomas Vivian
E. P. Willoughby

John A. Glasson
John Harris
Thomas A. Mitchell
Henry Pearce
Joseph S. Richard
Samuel Terrill
John Tregoning
Jane Vincent
William Walter

Class Leaders

Jacob Andrich
John Henwood
John Harris
James Carlyon
Edwin T. Tregoning

Thomas Vivian
William Tonkin
James Harry
Henry Tregoning
William Lanyon

Sunday School Superintendents

John Harris
Thomas A. Mitchell
William B. Martin
John Tregoning

Henry Tregoning
Thomas Morcum
William Lanyon
Samuel Pearce

Exhorter

James Carlyon

Organist & Choir Director

Emma Morcum Tregoning

Organist

Emily Collins Pearce

Trustees

W. H. Rogers	John Goldsworthy
V. B. Rexford	C. G. Harrison
J. Andrich*	Henry Tregoning
James Harry	Thomas Jeffrey
William Tonkin	John Pearce
John Dunstan	James Varcoe
William Gilbert	

Stewards

James Carlyon	James Harry
John Dunstan	Henry Tregoning
John Tregoning	Thomas Morcum
John Miners*	James Smith
Charles J. James	Edwin T. Tregoning
Emma J. Miners*	William Walters
Stephen Hatch	Alfred Tregoning
Thomas Trevarthen	John H. Bishop
N. R. Guy*	James Smith
John H. Pearce	William Lanyon
William Wedlake	Philip Bohemia
Samuel Pearce	William Pearce
F. H. Pascoe	A. Sunman*

These lists come from records kept by the church pastors from 1869 to 1881. As some kept better records than others, the lists are almost certainly incomplete.

*spelling uncertain

Appendix 3

THE NEW ALMADEN METHODIST-EPISCOPAL CHURCH — CLASSES

At New Almaden the class leaders in 1872 (under the Rev. Hazard) included John Henwood and Thomas Vivian. In 1873 William Tonkin, a miner and hoist operator, and John Harris, a miner, were the class leaders. In 1875 the following people belonged to Class number one, meeting at nine on Sunday morning, and led by Tonkin:

William Tonkin, widow	Ann Smith, married
William Nichols, married	John Harry, married
Mary Hodge, widow	William Pearce, married
Eliza. Penprays, widow	Leahariah Hall, married
Elizabeth Harry, married	James Fittz*, single
James Doble, widow	Sam. Henwood, married
Grace Gerrans, married	James Smith, married
John James	Samuel Pearce
John Pearce, married	Bridget Pearce, married
William Geach, married	John Tregoning, single
William Stiles, married	Wm. Goodman, widow
Richard Faull, single	John Gerrans, married
Charles James, married	John Capel, widow
Louisa Pearce, married	

In 1875 Class number three, led by James Carlyon, the miner and ex-horter, met at eight on Sunday morning:

James Carlyon, single	H. Tregoning, married
John Bennetts, married	John Davey, single
Harry James, single	Richard Hollow, single
John E. Barron	Wm. A. Morrish
John Dunstan, married	James Trengove
Stephen Hatch, married	Agnes Tregoning, single

In his book *The Cornish Jacks: The Cornish in America* (1969) Cornish historian A. L. Rowse estimated that 75% of the first generation of Cornish emgrants to the United States were illiterate. Some had learned to read in Methodist Sunday schools and others were self-educated. Captain James Harry's Thusday night classes at the New Almaden church were probably devoted to increasing adult literacy. In 1873 the class included the following:

Ann Smith	Mary Ann Pearce
Elizabeth Dunstan	Elizabeth Jeffrey
Eliza Pearce	Maria Bluett

In 1874 and '75 the class added

Emma Rouse	Susan Bunney
Caroline Mallet	Grace Tonkin
Caroline Phillips	Martha Jane Geach
Mary Hodge	Elizabeth Penprays
Eliza Ralph	Louisa Varcoe
Mary Hockey	Susanna Tregoning,
Susan Perry	Mary J. Goodman
Mary Harry	Maria Truscott
John Tregoning, Sr.	Bennett Perry
Richard Faull.	

While classes were a feature of the New Almaden church from the earliest days of its history until the end, few records of the classes have survived. Most pastors recorded only the names of the class leaders (see Appendix 2).

*spelling uncertain

Appendix 4

Probationers Record, 1872 - 1880

This is probably a partial record of those who attended class meetings on probation in order to become full members in the Methodist Episcopal Church. The record is from the years when New Almaden was part of the Los Gatos Circuit. Only the most committed Christians, united by regular attendance at class meetings, study and prayer, were received into the church in "full connection." They were the energetic nucleus of the Methodist church family. Many more, as many as 300 more, were received into the church in subsequent years. Some signed up as probationers more than once before finally being received. (Source: Los Gatos Church Record, 1869 - 1881, Archives, United Methodist Church, Berkeley).

1872 (Pastor Gafney) James Reutter

1873 (Pastor Gafney) Susan Bunny

1874 (Pastor Gafney) William Geach, John A. Bennetts, William L. Higgins, Martha Jane Geach, Mary Hodge (widow), William Pearce, Elizabeth Penprays (widow), William Pearce, Jr., Isacc Broad*, Eliza Ralph, Eliza Pearce

1875 (Pastors Gafney & Hopkins) Louisa Varcoe, Mary Hocking, Richard Faull, John Doble (widower), Stephen Hatch, Samuel Henwood, John Tregoning, Susanna Tregoning, William Mallet, Richard H. Hollow, John Gerrans, Grace Gerrans, Bennett Perry, Susan Perry, James Smith, Harry James, James Philips,

Stephen Tippett, Charles James, Maria Truscott, Mary Harry, Louisa Pearce, Jane James,

1876 (Pastor Hopkins) Ester Ann Eslick, Jane James, J. M. Evans, Mrs. H. S. Wilcox, Mary Ann Collins, Hannah Thomas, William Heathorne, Mary Heathorne, Elizabeth Mitchel, Emma Morcom, Samuel Argall, Matthew Willoughby, William Hicks, Constance Nichols, Jane Geach, Thomas Pascoe, Richard Ralph

1879 (Pastor R. W. Williams) Mrs. N. Gray, Mrs. Chegwin, Mrs. May, James Johns, Thomas Pascoe, Thomas Mathews, William J. Dunstan, Mrs. Dingle, Mrs. B. Hunsten*, Miss Thomas, Mrs. Rule, Peter Rule, Alfred Tregoning, John Doble

* spelling uncertain

Notes about Sources

In the interest of making this brief book as readable as possible, I have dispensed with footnotes and with a formal bibliography. In place of those I would like to offer the reader this description of my sources.

Mine Hill at New Almaden. Eye witness accounts of life at New Almaden included R. J. (Dick) Pearce, "Visiting My Old Home Town," an unpublished manuscript given to me by historian and author Clyde Arbuckle of San Jose. Another is "New Almaden Hill," by William J. Trevorrow, a manuscript loaned to me by Rear Admiral and Mrs. Ted Fredericks. *Contested Election Case of Frank J. Sullivan vs. Charles N. Felton from the Fifth Congressional District of the State of California* (1887, two volumes) was the source for quotations from Captain James Harry.

I also drew on the following newspaper accounts: San Jose *Mercury,* 14 April 1864, p. 2, col. 3, which tells of the first church building; William Gafney, "Los Gatos Circuit," California *Christian Advocate,* 16 Sept. 1875, p. 4; "Christmas Festivities at New Almaden," San Jose *Weekly,*" 6 January 1876, page 1; George E. Barnes, "A Thanksgiving Day Visit to New Almaden," San Francisco *Call,* 9 December 1883, page 1; and "New Almaden Memories of Bilingual Christmases," San Jose *News,* 23 December 1966, page 6.

Any population statistics in this book came from "The English Town Census," a research project sponsored by The New Almaden Quicksilver Park Association and The California Cornish Cousins. "The Census" has established that more than eighty per cent of the non-Hispanic population on Mine Hill were Cornish or of Cornish ancestry. From United States Census records, payrolls, rent-rolls, voter registration and burial records the project has documented the lives of more than 1,000 people who lived in the English-speaking camp between 1864 and 1912. I direct the project; Ruth Brown and John Faull are researchers; Russ Pearce is an adviser. The project is now scheduled for completion in 1998.

Wider background on New Almaden came from Jimmie Schneider, *Quicksilver: The Complete History of Santa Clara County's New Almaden Mine* (1992); and from Milton Lanyon and Laurence Bulmore, *Cinnabar Hills* (1967), a book primarily valuable for its photographs.

Russell Pearce, Dick Pearce's grandson, told me about the role of women in the building of the Methodist Church. His family, as much or more than any other, has preserved the stories of the old settlement. Jo Schneider Young, whose family has long been associated with New Almaden, read to me a description of the church fire from the journal of her pioneer ancestor, Charles Schneider. The post card mailed from New Almaden in the last days of the church is in the collection of John Drew, grandson of the last superintendent of the New Almaden mine. Clyde Arbuckle told me stories that he had collected from Dick Pearce and others. Doris Enman, granddaughter of Henry and Eliza James, told me stories of her family. Dr. Fred Harris, president of the Cornwall Methodist Historical Society, pointed out the uniqueness of the Thusday evening class. The original faded scroll inscribed by children to Mrs. Randol still hangs in the New Almaden Museum.

The Wesleyan background. The quotations from John and Charles Welsey are drawn from Rupert E. Davies, *Methodism*, Epworth Press, London, (1963, 1976, 1985). I have relied on several accounts of Wesley's life, especially Richard Heitzenrater's *The Elusive Mr. Wesley*, (1984, two volumes). I obtained further background from Albert Outler's *From Wesley to Asbury: Studies in Early American Methodism* (1976) and from *The Works of John Wesley*. Also helpful was R. E. Davies, *What Methodists Believe* (1988).

Background on Methodism in America came from Charles W. Ferguson, *Methodists and the Making of America* (1983); John G. McEllhenney, editor, *Proclaiming Grace & Freedom: The Story of the United Methodist Church* (1982); and Frederick A. Norwood, *The Story of American Methodism* (1974). Of wide value was *The Encyclopedia of World Methodism* (1974).

Methodist worship. I found the work of William Nash Wade essential to an understanding of worship practices during the era of the New Almaden church. His doctoral dissertation is "A History of Public Worship in the Methodist Episcopal Church and Methodist Episcopal Church, South, from 1784 to 1905," submitted to the Graduate School, Department of Theology, University of Notre Dame, Notre Dame, Indiana, March 1981. Also of value were two highly readable books, James F. White, *A Brief History of Christian Worship* (1993) and William H. Willimon, *Word, Water, Wine and Bread* (1980).

Cornish Methodism. Sources on Methodism in Cornwall included works by Thomas Shaw: *A History of Cornish Methodism* (1967);

Gwennap Pit: John Wesley's Amphitheatre (1992); and "St. Petroc and John Wesley: Apostles in Cornwall," Cornish Methodist Historical Association, Occasional Publication No. 4 (1962). Other valuable sources were John Pearce, editor, *The Wesleys in Cornwall* (1964); J. C. C. Probert, *The Worship and Devotion of Cornish Methodists* (1978); John Rowe, *Cornwall in the Age of the Industrial Revolution*, (1993, second edition); John Rowe, "Cornish Methodist and Emigrants," The Cornish Methodist Historical Association, Occasional Publications No. 11 (1967); and A. C. Todd, *The Cornish Miner in America* (1967).

Books that filled in the wider British background included Wellman J. Warner, *The Wesleyan Movement in the Industrial Revolution* (1930) and Robert F. Wearmouth, *Methodism and the Working-Class Movements of England, 1800-1850* (1937, 1947).

Local church history. The written records of the Los Gatos and New Almaden churches during the time of this history were found in "Los Gatos Church Record" (circa 1869-1881) at the archives of the California - Nevada Conference of the United Methodist Church, Berkeley; and in "The Church Record of the New Almaden Methodist Episcopal Church" (circa 1879-1912) at the archives of The History Museums of San Jose.

For information on Methodism in California I relied on C. V. Anthony, *Fifty Years of Methodism* (1901) and Leon L. Loofbourow, *In Search of God's Gold* (1950). Individual church histories were also important, including "A Century of Faith and Service, 1866-1966," published by First Methodist Church, Los Gatos; "The History of the Santa Clara United Methodist Church, 1846-1976 (1976); Ruth Rundle, *Soulsbyville United Methodist Church History* (1990); Estella L. Guppy, *Trinity Church, Advent 1860 to Easter 1903* (1903). I am indebted to the Rev. Loofbourow for the quotation from George Willis Read a medical doctor in Austin, Nevada, and for the story of the Methodist Mining Company. Also of value were George G. Bruntz, *The History of Los Gatos: Gem of the Foothills* (1983) and Clyde Arbuckle, *Clyde Arbuckle's History of San Jose* (1986).

Pastors & their wives. The California Conference Minutes, 1854 - 1914, provided most of the stories (as obituaries) of ministers and their wives. Other important sources were unpublished letters in the Methodist archives at Berkeley: W. B. Priddy letter to C. V. Anthony, circa 1901; Joseph R. Wolfe, letter to R. E. Wenk, circa 1903; John Walace Bryant to R. E. Wenk, circa 1903; Edwin Harry Smith, letter to the Rev. R. E. Wenk,

18 July 1904; F. J. Peters to the Methodist Historical Society, 1 April 1954. An account of Dr. Morrow's life was published as "A Minister Fallen," *The California Christian Advocate*, 18 April 1872. Edward Adams Hazen's biography, which provided much of the material for chapter 3, is *Salvation to the Uttermost* (1892).

In describing the lives of ministers' wives I referred to H. M. Eaton, *Itinerant's Wife: Her Qualifications, Duties, Trials, and Rewrds* (1851), reprinted in *The Nineteenth-Century American Methodist Itinerant Preacher's Wife*, ed. Carolyn De Swarte Gifford (1987). I also drew on Lillian Schlissel, *Women's Diaries of the Westward Journey,* (1982). The description of Hester Buxton (page 47) was written by the Rev. George Colliver.

Annotated version. An annotated manuscript with a bibliography (an earlier version of this work) is available in the Pioneer Papers, 1996, in the California Room of the San Jose Public Library.

Scriptural references. Though the New Almaden Methodists would have known the King James version of the Bible, they would easily recognize the passages of scripture used throughout this book, which were taken from the New Revised Standard Version (Cokesbury, 1990) and from the Book of Common Prayer of the Episcopal Church (1979).

Note on Terms

An English-speaking settlement: The Quicksilver Mining Company styled the English-speaking settlement on Mine Hill "English Town" and topographical maps show that name today. It was always a euphemism for a settlement that through much of its history did not have running water and never had a paved street. The author Mary Hallock Foote, who lived there, called it the "Cornish Camp." William Trevorrow, who grew up there, called it "English Camp," but said there were no English there — only Cornish. Lotty Tonkin and her sister Elizabeth Tonkin Colliver also remembered it as "English Camp." I have used the various names more or less interchangably and depending on the immediate context. The nearby Hispanic settlement was known as "Spanish Camp," a name that also designated the principle languaged spoken by the inhabitants.

Methodist circuits: To avoid confusion, one must distinguish a "Circuit" from a "District." A Circuit was the vaguely circular route traveled by an itinerant preacher. A District was a larger organizational unit, usually a geographical division, that groups several circuits and stations under the leadership of a presiding elder. Originally the Santa Clara Circuit was part of the San Francisco District, but in the mid 1860s it separated into a new, rather unwieldly Santa Clara District that extended all the way from Half Moon Bay to San Diego. This short-lived district disbanded when the Los Angeles District was formed in 1870, and the Santa Clara Circuit rejoined the San Francisco District. All of the districts were part of the California Conference, a yet larger unit, comparable (at least geographically) to a diocese in the Anglican or Roman Catholic churches.

New Almaden Quicksilver County Park - *Located twelve miles south of San Jose, the park includes the New Almaden National Historic Landmark District. New Almaden was the first site of mechanized mining in California. Number 1 indicates the main Almaden entrance to the park; number 2, the Mockingbird entrance; and number 3, the McAbee entrance. For information and details on riding and hiking trails, write the Santa Clara County Parks and Recreation Department, 298 Garden Hill Drive, Los Gatos, CA 95030 or the New Almaden Quicksilver County Park Association, P. O. Box 124, New Almaden, CA 95042.*

Index

Arbuckle, Clyde, 86

Baptism, 25-6, 72

California Conference, 28, 35-6,
 53, 77
California *Christian Advocate*, 29-
 30, 33, 59, 64, 66
Camp meetings, 23, 30
Catholicism, Roman, 27, 67
Centella Church (San Jose), 41, 77
Christy, S. B., 50
Church of the Brethern, 18
Cinnibar Hills, 61
Circuits, preaching, 22, 91
Class meetings, 54-56, 84-85, 86
College of the Pacific (see
 University)
Company store, 68, 69-70
Cornish people, 14-16, 19, 20-
 21, 52, 73
Cornwall (UK), 14, 19-21, 34, 55

Education, in Cornwall, 55
English Town (camp), 28, 91
Engle, Janet, 43
Episcopal Church, 71-72
Epworth League, 78

Family names
 Andrew, 60, Andrich, 82, 83,
 Argall, 30, 77, 78, 86, Barron,
 84, Bennett(s), 77, 78, 84, 86,
 Billings, 72, Bishop, 71, 83,
 Bluett, 55, 85, Bohemia, 83,
 Bulmore, 59, 61, 72, Bunny,
 30, 85, 86, Capel, 84, Carlyon,
 53, 82, 83, 84, Collins, 77, 86,
 Colliver, 61, 78, Cornish, 71,

72, Davey, 84, 86, Doble, 71,
72, 84, 86, Drew, 50, 66, 70,
71, 77, 78, Dunstan, 30, 55,
83, 84, 85, 86, English, 77, 78,
Eslick, 86, Faull, 14, 30, 71,
72, 84, 85, 86, Fittz, 84,
Gardner, 82, Geach, 30, 66, 84,
85, 86, Gerrans, 84, 86,
Gilbert, 83, Glasson, 82,
Goldsworthy, 56, 83,
Goodman, 84, 85, Gray (Grey),
51, 77, 82, 86, Guy, 83, Hall,
84, Hancock, 59, Harvey, 71,
72, Harris, 50, 82, 84,
Harrison, 83, Harry, 35, 50, 55,
66, 82, 83, 84, 86, Hatch, 83,
84, 86, Heathorne, 30, 86,
Henwood, 30, 82, 84, 86,
Hicks, 30, 67, 78, 86, Hockey,
85, Hocking, 78, 86, Hodge,
84, 85, 86, Hollow, 84, 86,
James, 30, 66-67, 71, 72, 77,
78, 83, 84, 86, Jeffrey, 55, 83,
85, Johns, 74, 77, 86, Kelly,
72, Lanyon, 52-53, 61, 82, 83,
Mallet, 85, 86, Martin, 82,
Miners, 56, 83, Mitchell, 29,
50, 77, 82, Morcum, 50, 74,
82, 83, 86, Morrish, 84,
Nichols, 30, 84, 86, Odgers,
60, Pascoe, 78, 83, 86, Paull,
72, Pearce, 25-26, 30, 50, 55,
66, 67, 70, 71, 74, 82, 83, 84,
85, 86, Penprays, 84, 85, Perry,
85, Phillips, 85, 86, Polglase,
77, Prisk, 82, Ralph, 85, 86,
Reed, 58, Rexford, 83,
Richard(s), 29, 50, 82, Rogers,
83, Rouse, 85, Smith, 84, 85,

93

94

About the Author

Gage McKinney is a member of the board of the New Almaden Quicksilver County Park Association and a lay reader in the Episcopal Church. He is currently president of Our Daily Bread, an ecumenical program that annually serves more than 35,000 hot meals to the hungry in Sunnyvale, California. He is also past president of the California Cornish Cousins.

McKinney has published widely. His historical articles have appeared in *The Californians, Cornish Worldwide, Forest & Conservation History* and other publications. He is a contributing editor to *The Merchant* and *Keltic Fringe* magazines. A previous work by McKinney on New Almaden won the California Pioneers' award for history. He also was the 1987 winner of the Montalvo Literary Arts Award for Excellence in Poetry.

In writing this account McKinney especially drew on the resources of the Archives of the California-Nevada Conference of the United Methodist Church, Berkeley and Stockton; the archives of the History Museums of San Jose; and the collections of the New Almaden Museum. He also conducted research at the Library of Congress, Washington, British Museum, London, and the Cornish Studies Library, Redruth, Cornwall. He and his wife, Ilka Weber, traced the routes of John and Charles Wesley through the west of England and Cornwall.

*Lamb and Flag - A Christian symbol of resurrection
and seal of Redruth, Cornwall, home of the author's ancestors.*